MESSY COOK

For Tatters

MESSY
COOK

Michael Raffael

PROSPECT BOOKS

2012

First published in 2012 by Prospect Books,
Allaleigh House, Blackawton, Totnes, Devon TQ9 7DL.

© 2012, text and photographs, Michael Raffael.

BRITISH LIBRARY CATALOGUING IN PUBLICATION DATA:
A catalogue entry of this book is available from the British Library.

Typeset and designed by Lemuel Dix and Tom Jaine.

The author, Michael Raffael, would like to emphasize that his fables are true fictions, and contain no covert allusions to real people, living or dead. Any resemblance to real people is entirely coincidental.

ISBN 978-1-903018-91-0

Printed and bound by the Gutenberg Press, Malta.

FOREWORD

Dear Reader,

Take a look at the cookbooks on your shelves: self-help recipe manuals, worthy advice from vegans and dieticians, ethnic collations, academic textbooks and spin-offs from TV series. Throw in the odd classic, the village fund-raiser and the oddity that slips past a publisher's marketing sniffer-dogs. There you have it.

If you picked this up, expecting any of the above, put it back on the shelf. It isn't a celebrity puff. It doesn't teach or preach. You won't be transported to exotic climes by the scent of lemon grass and kaffir lime leaves. It won't help you make the perfect soufflé or coddle a molecular egg.

This is a snapshot of what goes on in my kitchen. You aren't invited in as an overfed bluebottle-on-the-wall, but you're free to look, on the understanding that the picture is composed and selective.

Foodist gurus use four buzz-words to describe a cook's emotional engagement: 'Love', 'Passion', 'Craft' and 'Art'. This is *fine* for technically skilled, passionate lovers with an artistic bent. Most cooking happens as a day-to-day experience inside close relationships, family or a partnership, where the aim is or should be putting something on a plate for somebody who is hungry.

What – depends on who you are, how you live, what you like eating, your mood and any loose culinary nugget that the brain may dig up. Sometimes the result is great; usually it's edible. Every so often something goes wrong and it ends up in the bin.

Good cooking isn't a hobby to be picked up at weekends and shared around a dinner table. It's about habit and routine, adding the amount of salt that suits your taste, boiling the cabbage the way *you* like, not the way that famous chef tells you to like it. It's both personal and communal.

In the privacy of your own kitchen, you own your own thoughts, your own sensory reactions, your flawed ability and any tiny explosions of imagination you may have. Over time, and assuming you spend enough of it there, you become a cook with a unique fingerprint. Those clever French who still produce better food than Anglo-Saxons call it a *touche-personnel*.

When I was putting *Messy Cook* together, I showed a draft to an old friend who works at the deep-end of the media-cookery soup. Her response was: 'It's got a lot of words.' Well, 'Yes', it has. The question she should have to answer is: do bare recipes stripped of context have enough?

Chard, June 2012.

TABLE OF CONTENTS

washing up

When I bought it in a Bournemouth haberdasher's, it was a cheap, ugly, Japanese frying-pan. Thirty years on it's a thing of beauty. The outside is coated in a thick, black crust that flakes like a scab if I pick at it. Inside it has developed a dark patina. After using it, I may wipe it or rinse it, but never scrub it. Every so often I'll season it, coating the surface with oil and heating it gently for a while, a cast-iron massage that stops food sticking so that an omelette shakes, shimmies and flops over on itself: no trouble.

My family mocks my attempts at washing up, sometimes pissed off, sometimes pitying, more often frustrated that I can't perform the basic tricks of kitchen hygiene. They don't say it, but they imply that 'Cleanliness is next to Godliness', that I should care more, because glistening saucepans, they believe, are the secret of well-boiled cabbage. It's then that my thoughts flit to my favourite pan which taught me the craft of not washing up. Fussing over a missed smudge on a mixing bowl or mottled blotches on the blade of a carbon-steel knife or even a residual tide-mark in a pot is a false priority, a bit like the months of parsley chopping sadistic chefs used to inflict on young apprentices.

Although I'm notoriously bad at the job, it doesn't mean I don't know how it should be done. In fact, it's mainly cussedness on my part that I can turn this routine chore into a sequence of small failures. Inside me a little gremlin, possibly of French origin, says 'Non!' to excessive order and antisepsis.

Not that my system is quite without rigour. Plates, crockery and cutlery disappear in the dishwasher. A plastic suds-filled bowl stands on one side of the sink with a second bowl for rinsing in it. On the other side is the draining board. Dirties accumulate at one end, like sheep awaiting a dip. After they've passed through detergent and water baths they drip-dry, a random heap of culinary utensils ranging from food processors to skillets, skimmers, graters, tweakers, nickers and nippers.

How the pile ends up depends on its shape and volume at the front end of the production line. Perhaps, there should be an order: pans, then bowls, jugs, knives and hand-held gizmos, with the chopping board taking up the rear. Perhaps it would help to scrape or scoop out any detritus before starting: congealed gravy or maybe gobbets of two-day-old dried bread dough that are pebble-dashing the inner wall of a mixing bowl, the sticky jam at the bottom of a maslin pan. No doubt an experienced *plongeur* would instinctively know how to manage his load. In our kitchen, where meals don't operate to a timetable or follow a pre-ordained menu – no Sunday roast or Friday cod – the only rational response is: just cope, anyhow.

Washing-up liquids don't look the same. Some are blue, others green, yellow or orange, and their viscosity varies. It is an untested theory, but I suspect that they are made to an identical formula and only their concentration varies. An obsessive-compulsive might want to know whether two squirts of cobalt Own Brand equals half a squirt of emerald Brand X.

The density of a foam head brings no guarantee of potency. What does help is a pristine scouring pad. It gives the kind of satisfaction a man gets from a new razorblade. It obeys the same law of diminishing returns. The longer it remains in service, the less well it does the task for which it's intended. After a week, it grows limp. After a month it's a nasty rag to which unidentifiable bits of once-edible matter cling. Somehow or other, a false economy, it's never thrown out until it has all but disintegrated.

That palpable decay applies, suds-law, to the froth-topped water. Inevitably it converts into a greasy scum. At the outset scalding hot, it ends up tepid, turbid, no longer capable of cleaning anything. Whatever passes through is tainted with an invisible bacterial cocktail – which is also true of the assorted sponges and dish cloths involved in the business. Standing back, I can see a solution. Treat the whole thing like a game of two halves. Split the unwashed pile down the middle. Tackle half of it, chuck out the no-longer effective water and replace it with fresh. One of these days I might put this thought into practice.

Sieves, graters, potato mashers, cafetière plunger, even colanders (anything with holes or meshes) are hard to clean – almost impossible without a brush of some kind: a retired nail or toothbrush for the smaller meshes, something with bristles for pea-sized cavities. A pointed bamboo skewer can scratch out the stubborn whiskers of leek trapped in a Moulinette. It's also useful for unblocking sinks. (When it goes down the plughole, it bends a bit if it's jiggled; metal can't do this.) Such auxiliary equipment has to go somewhere, on the window-sill in my case, adding to the minimalist beauty of my kitchen.

Sooner or later any cook who keeps his or her knives sharp will slice a finger when scrabbling at the bottom of the bowl because the blade has been wedged between a rolling pin and the blender lid, edge upwards. The wound won't be life-threatening but it will bleed. With blood splashing everywhere, two-handed washing up ceases to be an option, but the one-handed method, like the Zen sound of one hand clapping, is a manual riddle with an unsatisfactory solution. More painful – it probably only happens once in a washer-up's career – is spiking something sharp and pointed under a finger-nail: ouch!

Custard left boiling on the stove will catch if it's forgotten for a few minutes – especially if it's made with cornflour. When this happens, it's tempting to scrape the burnt bit on the bottom with a wooden spoon. This is fatal. Black, charred flecks pepper the jealous yellow. A carbon back-taste renders the sauce unpalatable. To salvage it or limit the damage, you have to pour it into a fresh pan. Dealing with the black patch of carbonized starch, sugar, egg and milk (squirt of cream cleanser and a vigorous rub) classes as a first-degree burn, annoying but not serious.

Second-degree burns, the charred lumps sticking to the ribs of a contact grill, or third-degree burns, solidified blackjack caramel, take more elbow grease. Worst of all is the solid carbon crust formed because someone forgot the gently simmering pot of *sugo di pomodoro* or *cassoulet*. Overnight soaking, scratching with a palette knife and a can of oven cleaner will heal a fourth-degree burn, eventually, but making the effort to do it is a subliminal form of self-flagellation.

The draining board is a two-dimensional space designed for nomadic three-dimensional structures. At the simplest level objects spread laterally: utensils cradled in the appropriate space with dripping pans ranged upside-down beside each other. As soon as the ground floor gives out, stacking deteriorates into apparent anarchy. Jugs hang upside down on frying-pan handles, mixing bowls perch on casseroles, themselves lodged between other casseroles. Glass, metal and plastic jostle for a ridge or rim-hold. On a bad day, their arrangement resembles the contents of a skip at a recycling centre.

Despite its apparent disorder, the pile is satisfying. The whole thing has to be structurally sound, constructed of interlocking parts that only a qualified dry-stone-wall builder might notice. Finished, it symbolizes a *fait accompli*. It stays fixed until the components are unpicked to be put away in cupboards and drawers. The sheer volume, too, speaks of the effort spent on cooking. Each item, small or large carries the memory of a purpose, an action planned and executed. The odd smear or blotch that has been overlooked should not be thought of as 'dirty'. It's cookery's ectoplasm, spiritual proof of what happened on the other side.

The great chef, Auguste Escoffier, would probably disagree, but too much discipline or precision in a kitchen is suspect. Those who are obsessed by control, who want everything to be 'just so', should stick to hamburgers and French fries à la Big Mac. The ability to manage uncertainty distinguishes a cook at ease from one plodding worthily through a recipe. Someone with unhealthy thoughts about shiny saucepans isn't going to dip in his finger to taste the sauce. And if he doesn't do that, how can he care about its flavour?

If all this seems an excuse for shoddy workmanship, well perhaps it is – up to a point. Nobody will ever convince me washing up is a pleasure; it's a chore. It's something that has to be done quickly and, with luck, painlessly. Some people do it better than me. Good for them. My way suits me. It isn't – the obverse side of the coin – any guide to the way I cook.

artichokes backwards

Life is too short to suck bracts?

An artichoke in bloom, thistle-blue corolla flowering above overlapping, leathery scales has become an ex-vegetable, a pretty decoration to stand in a vase. Trace its life-story in reverse; it grows progressively more interesting.

One step backwards, before it bloomed, immature florets, protected by a shield-wall of outer petals (that aren't), covered its hairy tufted bottom. The candelabrum stem on which it perched was coarse and fibrous. It was the vegetal equivalent of a tough old boiler, edible – eventually.

Back off some more and it was a compact grenade that snapped off the stalk. Those who have struggled through 'artichoke *à la dinner party*' will have met it at this stage: pulling off bracts, dipping them in sauce and scouring them with incisors until they've worked their way to a bottom where they scraped away ticklish fuzz before eating the 'heart'.

This is the stage of maturity when professionals *turn* an artichoke, trimming it and paring it before rubbing it with lemon juice to prevent it discolouring.

But go back to the earliest, pre-pubescent stage when it was a freshly formed bud. The stem was still tender, the fluff undeveloped. Scatter a few of the outer leaves, petals or bracts over the kitchen-table, snip off the tops and the rest is good to eat either cooked or, when it's tiny, raw.

I'm starting to understand artichokes, even though they're not very English. One day, a bag of thirty-eight came back from our allotment: two or three varieties, some violet and spiky, some like chunky balls, some that should have been picked a fortnight earlier, some we should have left to grow a bit. They were all eaten, the best first, others frozen (not ideal, but practical) and a few chopped up, the hearts only, to go in a soup.

The overcooked bits made a mugful of *crema di carciofi*: a mashed sandwich-spread tarted up with olive oil and lemon juice. To cut back on waste, I rubbed the soft pulp from the bracts one by one, a job on emotional par with chopping parsley. A basinful of trimmings, peelings, pluckings and scrapings ended up on the compost heap for a few pounds of artichoke. For every mouthful eaten, three or four are thrown away unless you pick them very young.

A purely anecdotal observation: earwigs love artichokes. These scavengers treat them partly as food, partly as a convenient hideout for ambushing other insects and partly as home. The older the plant, the more it opens out, the more chance there is of finding two, three or even more lurking in the crannies. They have a talent for scuttling. In the kitchen, they'll dart from hiding as soon as the outer bracts are pulled off.

They aren't easy to drown, but they're not accomplished swimmers. The smart thing to do is heft freshly picked artichokes into a sink of water and the creepy-crawlies abandon ship.

This leads neatly into the task of handling these complicated thistles.

PREPARING ARTICHOKES

Before starting, have a bowl of cold water and half a lemon to hand. Watch out for the spiny ones. Check the stalks (they show how young or old the artichoke is); it affects cooking times.

As a guideline, pull off about three layers of bracts. This will leave purple artichokes looking like closed tulips and dumpy ones like a cross between *petanque* balls and grenades. Rub each one with lemon to stop the torn ends going black and drop it in water. What happens next depends on the ultimate use:

For baby artichokes, destined for *antipasti* – cut off the upper bracts about an inch above the bottoms and trim the stalks; you can split them in half lengthways or into quarters;

for plumper, larger but still firm and fresh ones – cut off the tops in the same way;

for hearts – trim away all the bracts, the fuzzy base that's often called the 'choke' and rub them all over with lemon again.

for older artichokes – don't do anything more; salvage what you can after they've cooked.

MARINATED ARTICHOKE BOTTOMS

150ml dry white wine • 200ml wine vinegar
500g artichoke bottoms • 200ml olive oil • 1 sprig thyme
1 sprig rosemary • 1 bayleaf • 1 garlic clove • 1tsp salt

Put the wine, 150ml vinegar and 300ml water in a pan. Boil and add the artichokes (halved or quartered if large). Simmer until just tender – check after 5 minutes – and drain. Heat 50ml oil. Add herbs and garlic. When the garlic colours take the oil off the heat and cool. Combine with the rest of the oil, salt and remaining vinegar. Bathe the artichoke bottoms in the marinade for a day or more.

POLPETTE WITH ARTICHOKES

3 *biscottes* soaked in milk • 1 egg • 100g grated onion
1tbs ketchup • 1tbs dark soy sauce • pepper
100g diced tomato • 150g cooked artichoke bottoms
500g minced pork • sunflower oil

Mix the *biscottes* (like rusks), egg, onion, ketchup, soy, pepper and tomato. Chop the artichokes into small cubes. Combine with other flavourings. Add the minced pork and knead well so the mixture is well blended. Divide into approximately 16 flattened meatballs. Fry in oil until browned on both sides.

ARTICHOKES AND COUSCOUS

150g chopped leeks • salt • 4 large artichoke bottoms
200g couscous • 100g butter • 150g diced smoked bacon
120g diced red onion • 2tbs chopped parsley
flaked Parmesan

Boil the leeks in 600ml salted water. Drain and slice them, but keep the water. Cook the artichokes in the same water until tender and drain them. Add a knob of butter to 200ml of cooking liquid and return to the boil. Rain in the couscous. Cover, take off heat and leave 5 minutes. Blanch the bacon 1 minute in the remaining cooking liquid and drain. Fry the bacon and onion in half the butter that's left and add the sliced artichokes. Coat the leeks in melted butter. Fold leeks, parsley, onion, bacon and artichokes into the couscous. If you've any sun-dried tomatoes to hand, add 2 or 3 chopped up.

ARTICHOKE DIP

3 large old artichokes • salt • 3 cloves garlic
100ml olive oil • 1 lemon • ½ seeded and diced small green chilli
2–3tbs mascarpone or fromage blanc

Cook the artichokes in boiling salted water for 25 minutes. After 15 minutes, add the garlic. Drain the artichokes and garlic. Use a teaspoon to scrape artichoke pulp off the bracts. Remove the fuzzy choke. Purée the bottoms and mix with the scrapings. Add crushed garlic, olive oil, lemon juice and chilli. Fold in the mascarpone. Add extra salt to taste.

asparagus

Buy a bunch of asparagus and the tightly fastened bundle contains calibrated spears: same length, same thickness. Those from the bed on our allotment poke from the soil, diverse and unpredictable. Wispy sprue, phallic spikes (some suffering from Peyronie's disease) and coy tips push upwards from a network of underground crowns. Gardeners state, with hundreds of years of lore to support them, that the harvest must never stretch beyond six weeks because it weakens the plants.

For us, a five-week surfeit of asparagus and hollandaise, asparagus vinaigrette, asparagus risotto, cream of asparagus soup, grilled asparagus with Parmesan and bits of asparagus thrown into any mish-mash that happens to be on the supper table is enough.

This annual superabundance gives us a changed perspective. We don't hold them in awe. They aren't a luxury. True, there's the excitement of the first taste – end of April, or early May, depending on the weather – followed by orgies when we pig out on them. This gives way to an experimental phase – arak instead of wine in a risotto, for instance. Then the thrill tails off.

One of those cookery 'rules' (nobody knows where it originated) is that the trimmed length of asparagus shouldn't stretch beyond the span of thumb and extended middle finger. This begs the question: 'What size hand?' Most chefs settle on twenty centimetres.

Ours can be upwards of a foot. Providing they fit our wok we'll cook them. This broaches the vexed question of how to boil asparagus. The triple-macaroon (Michelin used to award these, not stars) restaurant ideal is just long enough to make them crunchy. Tips that crumble are anathema. It's why special pans in which to stand them vertically are pragmatic. They work too when the diameter of each stem is more or less the same.

We cook our non-conformist pickings together, whatever their geometry. The result: butch, tumescent spears with plenty of bite alongside skinny, flaccid ones that slip down the gullet almost unnoticed. This affects their individual tastes too, in the same way that a carrot, say, boiled for half an hour won't be like one that's blanched. The lack of uniformity contributes to the pleasure. One is still green, almost raw and the other a wrung-out blend of unidentifiable vegetation.

It doesn't take a chemist to identify the musty taste of asparagus as sulphur (dimethyl sulphide actually). It's a defining character, one that sets it apart from other vegetables. Freshly cut, it's also sweet, but the natural sugars dissipate fast, within a day of harvest. This is long gone before Spanish or Californian exports reach the supermarket shelves. It's missing from the artistic tips garnishing restaurant plates.

Our ill-assorted bunches never hang around. We eat them straight away and although we don't boil them according to the book we don't compromise on freshness. Even if we are blasé enough to think of them as boring we'd never swap our ragbag crop for their overpriced, manicured sisters.

GREEN ASPARAGUS – THE BASICS

This is for mismatched, freshly picked spears, not calibrated bundles. The aim is to trim each spear, long or short, fat or thin, so it's edible from one end to the other. Pick a spot at the bottom where the white 'subterranean' end changes to green. Cut off the bottom with about 5cm green attached. Take a sharp potato peeler. Leaving the top 20cm untouched, pare around each spear down to the cut base. This will rid the asparagus of almost all its fibrous parts. Boil plenty of salted water in a wok. Drop the asparagus into it. Cook anything from 2 minutes to 10 minutes according to your preference. If you are just cooking very slender ones, even a minute may be enough. Drain either in a colander or, better, on a clean tea towel.

ASPARAGUS WITH RED ONION VINAIGRETTE

600g freshly boiled asparagus • lemon juice • salt
2tbs cabernet sauvignon vinegar • 50g diced red onion
8tbs olive oil

Leave the warm asparagus to drain 5 minutes. Squeeze a little lemon juice on the spears. Dissolve the salt in vinegar. Add the onion and whisk in the oil. Put the asparagus on plates and spoon the dressing over them.

ASPARAGUS AND FENNEL RISOTTO

80g butter • 100g finely diced onion • 220g Arborio rice
600ml hot, seasoned chicken stock • 2tbs arak [or any pastis]
500g cooked asparagus • 2–3tbs chopped fennel leaves
40g grated Parmesan

Melt half the butter in a saucepan and sweat onions until sweet. Add the rice and coat well. Pour over a third of the stock and cook, stirring, until the rice absorbs it. Repeat with a second third of the stock. Add the rest of the stock and the arak. Finish cooking rice, about 20 minutes. Add the asparagus, chopped into bite-size pieces. Fold in the rest of the butter, fennel leaves and Parmesan.

ASPARAGUS TABBOULEH

2tbs olive oil • salt • 200 g couscous
400g cooked asparagus • 1 red onion • 3 spring onions
200g cherry tomatoes • mint to taste
flat-leaf parsley to taste • 1 lemon

Boil 220ml water with salt and olive oil. Rain in couscous, boil again, cover and leave 5 minutes off the heat. Fork into a salad bowl and cool. Roughly chop asparagus. Slice red onions. Chop spring onions. Halve cherry tomatoes and season them. Shred mint and roughly chop parsley. Mix all the vegetables and herbs with couscous. Just before serving, squeeze plenty of lemon juice over the couscous.

ASPARAGUS MIMOSA

20 medium asparagus spears • salt • 4 eggs
1tsp Dijon mustard • chopped herbs to taste
2tbs tarragon vinegar • 2tbs olive oil
2–3tbs sunflower oil

Trim and pare asparagus bottoms. Boil in salted water keeping them a little firm. Drain and refresh with cold water. Cut each spear into three on the slant. Hard boil (10 minutes) eggs and shell them. Rub egg whites and yolks through a sieve separately. Season. Make a dressing with mustard, salt, vinegar and oils. Toss asparagus in dressing and sprinkle sieved egg over them.

vinaigrettes

Poet, playwright and novelist François Coppée floats forgotten in a backwater of literary history. His fifteen months (give or take) of fame date from 1869 when he wrote a one-act play *The Passer-by* which established the reputation of Sarah Bernhardt. Its success put him at the centre of a literary group called the 'Vilains Bonhommes' (Ugly Guys), named more for their dress-sense than personal looks. This band, which later included an under-age Arthur Rimbaud and Paul Verlaine, held monthly dinners at the Café des Mille Colonnes in Montparnasse.

It's tempting to believe that Coppée's only memorable quote originated at one of these thrashes. 'It takes,' he said, 'four men to prepare a salad: a profligate with the oil, a miser with the vinegar, a sage with the salt and a lunatic with the pepper.'

Over time, the aphorism has undergone a significant adjustment. The pepper has vanished and instead the loony's job, more appropriately, is to mix the whole thing together. He's the chief tosser.

What might have appealed to the poetic epicures was the paradox that vinaigrette, what Coppée was describing, contains very little vinegar. In fact, when it's at all assertive, there's too much of it. Salad creams and dressings disguise what they're coating. If they're tart or even tarty, no matter. Nobody attacks a Caesar salad because he can't resist iceberg lettuce. Vinaigrette is edible baby oil. Almost invisible, it clings to the leaves it coats in a fine film, a presence that helps them slide down into the digestive system.

On purely aesthetic grounds, Italians have more style: a squeeze of lemon juice, a generous splash of olive oil, a discreet dose of salt and the whole caboodle is tumbled together with the kind of energy that ensures each leaf, be it cos or corn salad is efficiently seasoned.

In our family, more from habit than any other culinary motive, we don't do it this way. Ours is a kind of half-way house between a dressing and vinaigrette. It respects the basics – five parts oil to one part wine vinegar, but introduces a little Dijon mustard and diced shallots. This is no more than what families across France do routinely, but it hasn't permeated Anglo-Saxon countries which are bent on tinkering with assorted balsamic or sweetened cabernet sauvignon vinegars, savoury mustards and recherché oils extracted from virgin sunflower seeds, argan nuts or whatever else can be sold as desirable, rare and expensive.

In defence of our nondescript approach, it's fair to add that the vinaigrette that goes on a lettuce isn't quite the same as one that goes on tomatoes (we'd mix in some basil) or with red cabbage (a little extra vinegar and red onions), or on warm leeks (extra shallots and enough mustard to emulsify the sauce). Nor do we always measure as scrupulously as we should if we were a bit more obsessive.

And there's a final aspect that's easily overlooked: the amount of vinaigrette in relation to what it's for. It's tempting to make half a cup or so, simply because most cooks measure with tablespoons, but this will often be overkill. An empty salad bowl shouldn't harbour an oily puddle.

POIREAUX VINAIGRETTE

12–16 trimmed 'pencil' leeks • salt • 3tbs tarragon vinegar
1tsp Dijon mustard • 2tbs diced shallots
12–15tbs sunflower oil

Cook the leeks in boiling salted water until just tender. Drain and press out excess moisture. Put a little salt and vinegar in a bowl. Add mustard and shallots. Whisk in the oil. Pour dressing over still warm leeks.

SPINACH AND COTTAGE CHEESE SALAD

salt • 1tbs wine vinegar • 10g Dijon mustard
4–5tbs sunflower oil • 220g baby spinach • approx 25g rocket
120g cottage cheese

Dissolve the salt in vinegar. Stir in the mustard; whisk in the oil. Toss the spinach and rocket in dressing. Divide between plates or salad bowls. Pile cottage cheese on each portion.

SWEET AND SOUR VINAIGRETTE

60g red onion • salt • 1tsp *cassis* mustard (or Dijon)
20ml cabernet sauvignon vinegar • 80ml sunflower oil
pepper

Dice the onion as fine as possible. Put it in a bowl with salt, mustard and vinegar. Stir to dissolve. Whisk in the oil and grind pepper into the dressing.

RED CABBAGE SALAD

600g red cabbage • 1 Cox's apple • salt
1tbs dry cider • 1tbs balsamic vinegar • 1tsp Dijon mustard
7–8tbs sunflower oil

Cut out the cabbage's core. Shred the cabbage as finely as you know how. Quarter, core and chop the apple. Dissolve the salt in cider and vinegar. Whisk in the mustard and oil. Toss the cabbage and apples in the dressing.

BROWN LENTILS

250g sliced onions • 60ml oil • 120g chopped streaky bacon
500g lentils • 1 chopped carrot • 250g tomato passata
1 stock cube • 2 bayleaves • sprig of thyme • salt and pepper

Sweat the onions in oil until softened. Add the bacon and cook out. Stir in carrot and tomato. Add lentils and enough water to cover – say 1 litre. Boil and add stock cube, bayleaves and thyme. Simmer until the lentils are tender. Adjust the seasoning.

LENTILS VINAIGRETTE

1 heaped tbs Dijon mustard • 2tbs vinegar • 7tbs oil
500g cold cooked lentils • salt

Beat the mustard, vinegar and oil together. Toss the lentils in dressing. Add salt to taste.

RIDGE CUCUMBER SALAD

500g ridge cucumbers • 60g whites of spring onions
2tbs salt • 1tbs white wine vinegar • 4tbs sunflower oil
2tbs chopped dill • pepper

Peel and slice the cucumbers. Slice the spring onions. Put cucumbers and onions in a colander. Toss in salt. Leave an hour to drain. Rinse and pat dry. Whisk vinegar and oil together. Add the dill and cucumber. Grind black pepper over the slices. (The picture below is the same salad but made with red, not spring onions.)

tomatoes from seed

Packets of seed collected at a car boot sale dictate the tomatoes we grow in our greenhouse every year: common varieties like Gardener's Delight or Shirley; fashionable ones like Brandy Wine; multi-coloured ones – Green Grape, Black Cherry, Sun Gold. If we continued planting different kinds every year for the rest of our lives, we'd only sample a fraction of the hundreds out there. When we go on family visits to France, we eat fleshy *marmandes* that split after rain, *olivettes* (thick-skinned, tart, plum-shaped) and the scruffy bush cherry tomatoes that flourish in the flinty Loiret soil.

The debate, under glass versus outdoor, based on subjective experience, seems ill-judged. People can get too precious. Enjoying what's to hand works better. Perhaps a sun-ripened organic San Marzano grown on the slopes of Vesuvius packs more punch. So be it. That doesn't mean the year's first tomato salad that travelled no further than the few metres from an English vine to a chopping board is inferior.

For a couple of summer months spilling over into autumn and the first frosts, tomatoes form a staple part of our diet. We eat them because they're there. It isn't a case of scratching one's head and trying to invent some mouth-watering twist on a twist of a classic recipe. Ripe is good enough. Most end up as salad. Softer, mushy ones may go into a soup or sauce. If there's a bumper crop we dry them until they're tacky and keep them as a seasoning.

That gives us a glut for less than a third of the year and nothing through the winter and spring. Then like everyone else blessed with a northern climate, we make do buying cans or Tetrapaks of processed tomatoes for cooking. What we won't waste money on is *fresh* tomatoes whether from the market or the supermarket. At their worst, one could swap them for a cabbage and blindfolded it would be hard to tell the two apart. The pick of the crop seem bland by comparison with our own produce. 'Seasonality' should be meaningful, not just a good intention that trips off the tongue.

Pa amb oli, a Mallorcan snack, has an exotic ring; 'Bread and oil', its translation, less so. In its understated way, it holds the key that unlocks the secret to all recipes with raw tomatoes. You split a fresh, perfumed tomato in half and sprinkle sea salt over it. Next you rub it over a chunk of bread, not so much that the juices turn it pappy. Then you splatter cold-pressed olive oil on top, not a harsh peppery one, one that's more golden than green and tastes of ripe fruit.

Yes, we all know about the synergies of tomato and basil. Without the salt it's a loveless marriage. And the bread? Can anyone who eats a tomato salad resist mopping up the juices on his plate with it? Imagine the Mediterranean diet without tomatoes and at the same time imagine the Mexican diet without olive oil. Now there's a thought on which to ponder.

HALF-DRIED TOMATOES

1kg cherry tomatoes • 20g salt • 20g vanilla sugar
pepper • 2tsp *herbes de Provence*
1tsp powdered dried orange peel (optional)

Halve the tomatoes. In a bowl, mix them with the other ingredients. Leave them on a rack or sieve to drain for 4 hours. Dry them in an electric dehydrator for 6 hours. Store in a sealed container.

CHEDDAR AND TOMATO GRATIN

600g fleshy tomatoes • 150g grated vintage Cheddar cheese
2tbs basil purée or torn basil • black pepper
60g fresh breadcrumbs

Slice the tomatoes. Layer them in a small gratin dish with 100g Cheddar. Spread basil on top and season with black pepper. Preheat oven to 200°C. Mix the breadcrumbs and remaining cheese. Sprinkle over the tomatoes. Bake 30 minutes.

MIXED TOMATO AND FETA SALAD

500g assorted tomatoes • salt • 1tbs wine vinegar
5tbs olive oil • 1tbs basil purée • black pepper
30g diced red onion • 20g spring onion rings
150g cubed feta

Roughly chop the tomatoes and sprinkle salt on them. Leave 30 minutes. Dissolve a little more salt in wine vinegar. Whisk in olive oil and basil purée. Add pepper and onions. Toss tomatoes and feta in the dressing.

TOMATO SAUCE

1.5kg ripe, fleshy tomatoes • 3 tomato pedoncules • basil stalks
1tbs dark brown sugar (optional) • 2tbs olive oil • salt

Halve the tomatoes. Put them in a non-reactive pan with pedoncules (i.e. the stalks) and basil. Add brown sugar if you decide to use it. Simmer very gently for at least one hour. (Add water if reducing too fast.) Pass the sauce through a mouli into a bowl. Empty it back into the pan. Add olive oil and reduce until thick. Season with salt.

PICKLED NASTURTIUM SEEDS

Pick the seeds as soon as the flowers die. Wash them thoroughly. Toss them in coarse salt. Leave in a colander overnight. Rinse and pat dry. Empty them into a jar. Pour boiling white wine vinegar over them. Seal and leave a month in a dark place before opening. They're crunchy and more interesting than commercial capers.

SPAGHETTINI, TUNA, NASTURTIUM SEEDS

120g diced onion • 40ml olive oil • 2 crushed garlic cloves
250ml fresh tomato sauce • 1tbs basil purée • salt and pepper
2tbs pickled nasturtium seeds • 150g canned tuna
400g *spaghettini*

Sweat the onions in oil until soft. Add the garlic. Pour on the sauce. Simmer about 15 minutes. Season with basil, salt and pepper. Fold in nasturtiums and tuna. Cook the pasta in boiling salted water and drain. Leave a splash of water in the pan. Add back the pasta and then the sauce. Toss until well coated.

rata...........touille

Ratatouille never jumped from the womb ready-formed. It's a shape-shifter that changes ingredients and quantities ad infinitum. The name itself snaps into two: *rata*, something that failed, a mess, and *touille*, (from *touiller*, to stir). Provence is its foster-home, not its birthplace. The heroine of a Zola novel about alcoholism was dishing it up in a Paris tenement 150 years ago, decades before it reached the kitchens of Marseille.

Its uncertain roots explain why it never settled down. 'The secret is to cook each vegetable in a separate pan, so they are all perfectly cooked,' or 'Stew it long and slow until all the flavours come together,' or 'Keep it crisp and al dente'. Over time, I've made it every which way, with or without aubergines and/or peppers, in a single casserole or in three separate *sauteuses*. On impulse, I've added bacon (its earliest incarnation may have contained scraps of meat) or potato (*patatouille?*).

The only imperative is that the end-product tastes good, though, granted, this begs the issue of what 'good' means. Defining it by its opposite dodges the question, but helps. An under-ripe tomato off a British supermarket shelf in January doesn't cut it, neither does old sprouted garlic nor dried basil tasting of teabags. Biodynamic aubergines, olive oil from Nyons and fresh-picked, finger-length courgettes have an emotional pull; they won't tip the scales one way or the other.

Quantities? Proportions? Ratatouille needs no measuring jug, no set of scales, no instructions advising 'cut into quarter-inch rings' and 'fry for four minutes in hot oil, then turn', but it has a kind of structure. Onions, quartered and sliced with a sharp knife that cuts not bruises are the mortar holding it together. The other vegetables are the bricks.

This is where the business end starts. A wok is more practical than a pan, especially for the *touille* part. The oil should be hot enough to fizzle when the onions go in, but not enough to satisfy a Chinese hawker. They have to fry, not boil, until they're soft and a little sticky. That's when I take them out and set them aside.

There should be some oil left. If there isn't, I'll splash in a bit more. As soon as it's very hot, almost smoking, it's the turn of the sliced peppers and chopped courgettes.

When chefs sauter, they toss the contents of a pan into the air. It looks impressive, but cools the oil and food. What works for me is to leave well alone until the smell of browning vegetables wafts upwards. Then, I'll turn them and fry them some more. My aim isn't to cook them through, so I'll empty the wok again to make room for the aubergines, never bothering to salt these first as some French do.

Aubergines, eggplant, are greedy. They soak up oil and store it like fat tenors holding their breath until they're cooked; then ooze it out again. They don't deserve the excess oil they cry out for. Once their skins start to wrinkle, I add back the onions, courgettes and peppers. That's the moment to turn down the heat and mix in garlic crushed with salt.

What kind of tomatoes and how many depends on mood, or on the time of year. If they're plump and fleshy, it does no harm to be extravagant. When they're acid or out of a tin, they don't contribute that much apart from moisture. More often than not a spoon of brown sugar comes to the rescue to counteract their tartness.

How the *rata* turns out depends on what the cook does next. Over a minimal heat, carefully stirred for an hour or longer, it will stew gently to a thick, vegetal compote in which all the flavours blend together. At the other extreme, by firing up the gas and moving the contents of the wok around, it takes just a few minutes to end up with textured, courgettes, peppers, aubergines and onion in a fresh tomato coulis.

Herbs are cosmetics: foundation and highlights. Sprigs of fresh thyme or basil stalks act as the former. *Herbes de Provence* are the heavy coating of mascara on false eyelashes. Basil leaves sprinkled over the top are wasted garnish. Too many mixed in a ratatouille can make it as blowsy as an over-perfumed old tart.

GREEN TOMATO RATATOUILLE

100ml olive oil • 350g sliced onions • 400g courgettes
3 crushed garlic cloves • 400g chopped 'Green Grape' tomatoes
salt and pepper • 1 tbs basil purée or leaves

Heat half the oil in a skillet or sauté pan. Cook the onions slowly until they're transparent and browning. Take them out of the pan and reserve. Chop the courgettes into bite-sized pieces. Pour the rest of the oil in the pan and turn up the heat. Sear the courgettes so they colour. Stir in the garlic. Return the onions to the pan together with tomatoes. Stew gently until the courgettes are cooked through. Season with salt and pepper. Finish with basil.

RATATOUILLE

100ml olive oil • 150g sliced onions • 4 crushed garlic cloves
300g courgettes, bite-sized pieces • 150g red pepper, sliced
300g aubergines, bite-sized pieces • 400g tomato
basil, leaves and stalks • salt and pepper

Heat 30ml oil in a pan or wok. Sweat the onions until soft. Add the garlic and cook two minutes more. Empty the onions and garlic into a fresh pan. Fry courgettes and red pepper in oil until coloured. Add to the onions. Fry aubergines in oil until coloured. Add them to the onions, etc. Chop up the tomatoes. Add them and basil stalks to the pan. Season and simmer very gently for an hour. If the ratatouille is watery, reduce the liquid. Stir in basil leaves.

VEGETABLE SALPICON

70ml olive oil • 100g diced onion • 100g artichoke bottoms, cubed
100g courgettes, cubed • 2 crushed garlic cloves • 8 baby carrots
200ml tomato passata • salt and pepper
2 tomatoes

Heat the oil in a skillet or sauté pan. Fry the onions, artichoke and courgettes until coloured. Add the garlic and carrots. Pour over the passata and season. Stew without boiling, about 20 minutes. Blanch tomatoes in boiling water for 12 seconds. Skin, core, dice and season. Fold into vegetable mixture and serve. This is good with pasta.

pesto

Growing basil from seed is easy, one of those herbs that can be left on a window ledge, watered every so often and pillaged for its leaves. And there are different kinds too, spiky leafed bush basil, Flopsy-Bunny-eared basil, holy basil and purple basil. None of these has the intensity of Genoese basil. Pulled up by the roots and bunched is how they sell it in Ligurian markets.

That's a luxury beyond the scope of the English summer, but for two or three months we have more than we need so long as we nip the leaves off the stems with care and stop the plants from flowering. When it's time for a pesto blitz, we can fill a couple of colanders, enough to support a cottage industry or neighbourhood trattoria had we the inclination. Give it away, fill sandwiches with it, eat it with a spoon, we've done it. There must be oxidized, vintage blocks of pesto lost in the freezer dating from the heyday of Mrs Thatcher.

The name 'pounded' is a give-away isn't it? It takes hours bashing, bumping and grinding with pestle on mortar to pulp that quantity of leaves. It's true that gadgets will chop or liquidize the leaves, but the taste and texture never turns out the same. Perhaps it's because, by hand, we start off with coarse salt in the mortar that helps to bruise the leaves while breaking them down. Then there's the intangible reward for putting in all the effort.

Stirring leaves blended in a processor into a half-finished batch in the mortar before adding the garlic, pine kernels, olive oil and cheese is more of a compromise than a cheat. After a morning spent bashing it can seem a tempting option. The alternative is to forget about *pistou* or *pesto* and whizz up the basil with garlic, salt and oil in the Magimix. Packed in sterilized jars and stored in the fridge it's a condiment that lasts through the cold months.

What to do with pesto isn't a problem in itself. It's so potent that it calls the shots whether it's being added to a soup, tossed with most shapes or styles of pasta or mixed with any recipe that includes the word *pomodoro*. It's good lengthened with mascarpone, no worse served as little concentrated flavour blobs in which to dip a prawn. Basically, it's a 'Get out of jail' card, a twenty-first-century equivalent to the tomato ketchup bottle.

The jars of basil paste/purée in the fridge are something else. Of course it's blander, but it still has more punch than other winter herbs. Compared to dried basil that tastes like the content of recycled teabags it's worth having. Spooned into soups and stews or beaten into mashed potatoes just before serving, it brings its distinct hot-climate aroma to cold evenings. Treated as a seasoning, it lifts salads, even unlikely combinations like coleslaw. The only danger, assuming that one has made more than is strictly necessary, is that it will turn into a stop-gap, a routine seasoning, a household cliché that steals into dishes where it has no legitimate right to be.

PESTO OR PISTOU

1tsp coarse salt • 60g basil leaves • 10g garlic
30g pine kernels • approx. 60ml olive oil
60g grated Parmesan

Put the salt in a large mortar and pound a handful of basil. When it's mashed, add another handful and continue. Once all the basil is bruised, continue pounding it. Add the garlic and crush it. Add pine kernels and continue pounding. Start adding olive oil to the mixture, but continue pounding. Stir in the Parmesan when the basil is fragmented. Don't worry about bits of pine kernel. Store in a sealed jar in the fridge.

BASIL PURÉE

1 colander piled with basil leaves • 100ml olive oil
1tsp salt • 3 crushed garlic cloves

Sterilize and cool a jar large enough for the purée, say 500ml. Put the basil, 85ml olive oil, salt and garlic in a processor. Blend to a purée. Fill the jar with it and cover with remaining oil. Seal.

BEIGNETS SOUFFLÉS AU PISTOU

50g butter • 320ml water • 75g flour
2 eggs • 50g pesto • frying oil

Heat the butter and water in a smallish pan. Boil. When they come up the sides, rain in the flour. Stir until smooth. Cool for 5 minutes. Beat in the eggs one by one until glossy. Beat in the pesto. Heat frying oil in a wok until moderately hot – less than for chips, but still sizzling. Using two teaspoons, drop nuggets of dough in oil. Fry until golden, turning as necessary. Drain on kitchen paper. Serve very hot.

Cheddar cheese and 2tbs basil purée instead of pesto is a good alternative.

small fry big fry

Conservationists frown on whitebait and they may be right. Tiny herrings, they're much too small to catch, aren't they? The point isn't so much what they are as what to do with them. Fried they belonged on the menu of London's regional and seasonal cookery. Then, thanks to the deep-freeze, they spread around the country. There's no apparent skill to preparing them: dip them in milk, flour and deep-fry them until 'crisp'. It's this last word that throws everything up into the air. With whitebait it means brittle enough to snap in half, not golden on the outside and tender under the skin. There's a logic behind this too. The fishlets still contain their brains, eyes, guts and their bones. It's not something one wants to dwell on when plugging one's mouth with them. Crunch and swallow; don't chew.

Harmonizing the outside with the inside is the secret of all frying shallow, deep or in a wok. Heston Blumenthal did not invent the technique of triple-cooked chips (blanching in water, then double-frying them), manufacturers were doing that already. What he did was customize his design, from the mealiness of the potato, to the size of the chip and its crispness. His eyes-wide-open approach is what any cook should aspire to – if not supported by science then based on the back-story of accumulated experience.

My sweet and sour pork recipe, heavily stained, is on page 133 of Pei Mei's *Chinese Cook Book*, volume 1. Setting aside the sauce, the critical part is what happens to the meat. It's cut in pieces, marinated and then, just before frying, coated in cornflour. The method continues: 'fry pork until brown and done (about 2 minutes), take out, reheat oil then fry once more until crispy.' Almost perfect! What's missing are details that only emerge by trying the dish over and over again: controlling the heat of the oil; not frying all the pieces at once, but doing them in batches; giving them a final fry-up so they're all equally hot and crusty.

If the pack-horses of frying are the quantity and temperature of the oil or fat, its quality matters just as much. It's something Japanese cooks with their passion for freshness understand. No tempura batter ever tasted stale. Indian cookery would be impoverished without its *tadka*, spices and aromatics fried in ghee that are folded into daals, meat and vegetable dishes to add their fragrance. Now, think of the reek in the street outside a bad chippie, or the way rancid oil smells waft around a house, clinging to walls and curtains.

Because it's always 'fast food', it ought to be easy. After all, Mc D doesn't hire intellectuals. Is it though? Choose the wrong kind of potato and French fries turn out flabby, whether double or quadruple cooked. Bacon pumped full of water stews in its own juices. Batter looking golden and appetizing in the pan is thick and leathery on the plate, despite the beer that went into its formulation. Boiling in oil produces some of the nastiest food on the planet.

PRAWNS IN PERRY BATTER

125g flour • 80g cornflour • 300ml ice-cold perry
about 1 litre sunflower oil • 600g large, raw, shelled prawns

Sift the flour and 30g cornflour. Whisk in 200ml perry. Leave 5 minutes. Fold in the rest of the perry. Heat the oil in a wok. Dust the prawns with remaining cornflour. Dip them in batter, or two at a time. Fry until crisp and drain on absorbent paper.

The oil is ready for frying when the surface shimmers and a drip of batter rises to the surface at once and sizzles.

DARK RUM FRITTERS

175g self-raising flour • 80g caster sugar • 2 eggs
2tbs dark rum • 75g softened unsalted butter • frying oil
1tsp ground allspice

Mix the flour and 50g sugar. Work in beaten eggs and rum. Cream the butter and work into the batter (an electric mixer makes this easier). Roll out the dough on a floured surface. Cut into 24 pieces. Heat enough oil in a wok to fry them. Fry in hot, not smoking, oil until golden. Drain on kitchen paper. Dust with remaining sugar and allspice.

FRIED PORK – FOR SWEET AND SOUR

500g pork spare rib • pinch salt • 2tsp light soy sauce
1 egg yolk • 120g cornflour • frying oil – about 1 litre.

Bash the meat with a rolling pin to tenderize it. Cut into rough cubes of 2–3cm. Make a sticky marinade with soy, egg yolk, 1tbs cornflour and 1tbs water. Coat the meat in marinade and leave for at least one hour. Spread cornflour on a tray. Heat the oil in a wok. Coat each piece of pork in cornflour. Fry a few pieces at a time until coloured. Drain and reserve. Check the oil is very hot and refry the pork until crisp. Drain on absorbent paper. Coat with sweet and sour sauce.

SWEET AND SOUR SAUCE

1tbs cornflour • 3tbs wine vinegar • 4tbs soft brown sugar
4tbs Heinz tomato ketchup • 90ml water • 1tbs oil
100g chopped fresh pineapple

Make a paste with cornflour, vinegar, sugar, ketchup and water. Heat the oil in a wok. Fry the pineapple until it colours. Stir in the other ingredients and heat only until it has thickened.

CHEESE AND POTATO PANCAKE

100g fatty streaky bacon • 400g peeled potato
100g grated Cheddar

Dice the bacon. Render the fat in a non-stick pan. Slice the potatoes (think a 50p coin). Add them to the pan. Coat them in bacon dripping. Cover the pan. Turn down the heat. Cook the potatoes until they soften, about 15 minutes. Part-crush them with a fork. Mix in the cheese. Turn up heat and fry until the bottom is crisp. Flip the pancake cooked side up on a large plate. Slip the pancake back in the pan to crisp the other side. Turn out.

off the top of my head

Pull a rabbit out of a hat and it's just a rabbit. Pull a hat out of a hat, and another hat out of that hat and then, maybe, a rabbit. That's creative. In the kitchen, imagination is second nature, less of the 'What can I do to blow them away', more of the 'Bit more salt', 'Extra teaspoon of honey'. It doesn't have a rule book. More often than not it's invisible. Dish something up and it seems totally familiar, ordinary whether it is or whether it's not. It isn't puffed up, attention seeking. It's not furry and it doesn't have long ears.

Mostly it's about reacting. The lettuces in the garden have started bolting. Left, they'll turn bitter, but the more tender leaves at the top are still good enough for a soup. Rather than throw out the green leek tops, mix them with some mashed potato. What kind of ice-cream would the porridge left over from breakfast make, perhaps with a sprinkling of cinnamon? Hey, there's still a piece of camembert in the fridge: 'Frog rarebit?' This isn't systematic, planned cuisine. You just do it, *e basta*.

It's also opportunistic. So the larder is bare except for some Charlottes, *haricots verts*, half a packet of smoked salmon and a jar of pickled cucumbers. The kind of cook likely to face this situation should be able to produce something edible. Performing professional chefs don't own the franchise for transforming them into a televisual masterpiece. Once you know how to fry an egg, you don't take a course to learn how to grind a peppermill over it. Far too many recipes act as culinary Zimmer frames for those who don't need them.

In the privacy of his or her own kitchen anyone should feel

comfortable taking a chance. Substitute 'tweak' for 'invent' and you have the secret of a thousand cookery-writing, recipe-compiling careers. A tablespoon of soy sauce in the Lancashire hotpot, a shredded lovage leaf in the prawn cocktail, fizzy cider instead of beer in the batter: it's not hard.

The premise for tinkering is that the game's worth the candle. Braising artichokes in strawberry jam may be a unique experiment; it isn't most people's idea of the ideal snack. Adding some artichoke bottoms that have been languishing in a freezer to a couscous can't do any harm. Ground almonds mixed with the sponge base of a steamed pudding actually improves the texture. It is a technique that's been around for over 150 years, but when you happen upon it by chance and give it a whirl and discover it's better than what you've been doing until then, you have every right to enjoy a eureka moment.

Once you've learnt how to cook well enough, once a few techniques are second nature, tricking things out off the top of your head becomes a game, something to do because you can do it. Of course, things can go wrong. It isn't for the self-conscious, but risk is an addictive spice to add to the business of cookery.

GRATED BEETS

600g large beetroot • 40g butter • 1–2tbs soy sauce
2tbs toasted pine kernels • 1tbs finely diced shallots

Put the beetroot in a pressure cooker with a pint of water. Cook 45 minutes, drain and peel off the skin. Grate coarsely with a cheese-grater. Squeeze out as much moisture as you can. Melt the butter in a pan. Toss the grated beet in it. Stir in the soy sauce. Fold in toasted pine kernels and shallots.

CELERIAC AND CARROT RÉMOULADE

1 large celeriac • ½ lemon • 120g peeled carrot
70g mayonnaise • 10g Dijon mustard
1tsp mustard seeds

Peel the celeriac and drop the pieces into water and lemon juice. Shred the celeriac and then the carrot through a vegetable grater. Combine the mayonnaise and mustard. Fold the vegetables into the mayonnaise. Dry-fry the mustard seeds until they start popping. Sprinkle over the rémoulade.

A VERY ENGLISH RISOTTO

200g diced onions • 40ml sunflower oil • 1tbs tomato purée
200g Arborio rice • 600ml hot seasoned chicken stock
50ml Cinzano • 4 cooked artichoke bottoms • 2 egg yolks
80g grated vintage Cheddar

Sweat the onions in oil until they're transparent. Stir in the tomato purée, then the rice. Cook gently for a couple of minutes. Add a third of the stock and boil until absorbed. Repeat with a second dose of stock. Add the remaining stock and Cinzano. (Cooking takes about 20 minutes.) Slice or chop the artichokes and fold into the rice. Beat the yolks with a tablespoon of water and beat into rice. Fold in grated cheese.

SCOTCH PANCAKES

200g flour • 15g baking powder • 100g caster sugar
pinch of salt • 2 eggs • 30ml lemon juice
150ml milk • 70g melted butter

Sift flour and baking powder twice. Add sugar and salt. Lightly beat eggs and lemon juice. Make a well with flour and add the egg. Work in the egg adding a little milk at a time to obtain a smooth batter. Fold in 40g butter. Heat a cast iron griddle. Brush with melted butter. Drop a tablespoon of batter, per pancake, onto the griddle. When it puffs up and starts bubbling flip it over. Cook until set. Serve with honey, jam or maple syrup.

BOLTED LETTUCE SOUP

1 bolted cabbage lettuce • 50 g butter • 1 diced onion
200g diced potato • 600ml chicken stock • salt
5 mint leaves

Check the lettuce leaves aren't bitter. Roughly shred about 200g of them. Melt the butter in a pan and sweat onion until it starts to soften. Add potato and cook a couple of minutes more. Pour over the stock, boil, season and add mint leaves. Add the lettuce and simmer for a couple of minutes. Liquidize the soup.

CLEMENTINE MARMALADE

1 kilo clementines • 1tsp sunflower oil
1tsp lemon juice • 1 kilo jam sugar
2 passionfruit (optional)

Wash clementines to remove traces of preservatives. Peel and shred the peel thinly. Blanch shredded peel 6 minutes in boiling water. Chop fruit into small pieces over a bowl to retain juice. Put all the ingredients in a pan. Bring to the boil, stirring to dissolve the sugar. Boil 6 minutes hard. Pour while hot into sterilized jars. A variation which you may choose to follow is to add the juice and seeds of two passionfruit.

—

SOUP IN A HURRY

1 diced onion • 500g potato chopped small • 2–3tbs bacon dripping
2 stock cubes • 500g diced leek • 200g grated carrot
2 tbs basil purée • salt and pepper

Sweat the onion and potato in bacon dripping until they start to soften. Add 2 litres boiling water, stock cubes, leek and carrot. Simmer until the leeks are done, about 10 minutes. Stir in the basil purée, 'Zoom!' in the blender, and check the seasoning.

SYRUP PUDDING

175g softened butter • 150g caster sugar • 150g flour
15g baking powder • 150g beaten egg • ½ tsp almond essence
30g ground almonds • 150g golden syrup

Grease a two-pint pudding basin with 25g butter. Cream the softened butter and sugar. Sift flour and baking powder. Combine half the egg with the creamed mix. Add a couple of spoonfuls of flour. Incorporate. Beat in the rest of the egg and essence. Fold in the ground almonds. Melt the syrup in a pan and pour into the pudding basin. Add the sponge mixture. Cover with foil plus elastic band. Steam in a saucepan of simmering water for two hours. (The water should be half way up the basin's sides.) Add extra hot water to the pan if necessary. Turn out the pudding.

balletjes

Dutch for 'meatballs', the title was chosen with care. It sidestepped evocative *polpettine*, not-so-sexy rissoles and the sober-but-helpful 'Things to do with mince.' Ground-up animal protein, edible hardcore, fills the gaps when menu planning falls down a hole. Just because it's cheap, because it takes disparate chunks of flesh and mangles them together, because it's the butcher's way of offloading bits that might otherwise be binned, because it disguises a cocktail of flesh, fat and gristle or because it doesn't raise any expectations, that doesn't mean it's degraded food. In pre-mincer, pre-food-processor cultures, where chopping meat by hand, sometimes to a paste, enhanced its status, the reverse was true. Luknow's *galuti kabab*, the delight of the Indian city's nawabs, could pass for a spiced-up Big Mac. Greek *keftedes*, flavoured with mint, oregano and onion, were once a dish fit for Lord Byron's table (not really – he was vegetarian).

By themselves meatballs aren't things of beauty. It's the cook's imagination that adds value – makes them respectable. They may be coarse or dense, meaty or softened with breadcrumbs, held together with egg, the size of a cricket ball or a peanut, totally bland, fiery, an admixture of anonymous flesh (pork with beef is good), lean or fatty, fried, grilled, dropped in a soup, wedged in a bun, tossed with pasta, thrown together or dosed with chemical precision. Exclusively round? Of course not! Hockey puck, bar skittles cheese, torpedo, diminutive rock cake, briquette: more or less any shape goes.

Mince isn't puffed up. It never puts pressure on the cook. Egon, the one-eyed Legionnaire chef, serves Beau Peep dinner in the eponymous comic strip: 'Food,' he says, 'should be an experience, an adventure, a treat for the senses.' The next picture shows him holding up a bucket: 'How many handfuls of mince do you want?' That's the right approach.

The wrong one? I had a friend who would cook, word for word, Robert Carrier's recipe for Bolognese sauce for lunch parties: onions, garlic, carrots, celery, herbs, red wine, cream and mince, spurious high-class nosh. It wasn't so much bad as unnecessary. Half the cost and half her effort would have produced something better.

It may be a stop-gap, something knocked up in a hurry. It may be something like a *ragú* that seems to improve the longer it simmers on the side of the stove. The only determinant is that it tastes OK. Not everything we eat has to be memorable, worth recording. It's enough that those who eat it will enjoy and move on.

Good meatballs should be like one-night stands, nice enough but forgettable with no threat of indigestion. Their attraction lies in the unexpected spice or herb, the kick it may give. They don't have to stand up to scrutiny. In our home we refer to them as 'bollocks', a light-hearted deformation of *balletjes*. It's an affectionate term that puts them into perspective.

MEAT BALLS – FOR SOUPS

100ml olive oil • 200g finely diced onion • 250g minced beef
250g minced pork • 3tbs finely diced black olives
30g egg white (1 small egg) • 1tbs soy sauce • 1tbs tomato ketchup
salt and pepper • flour

Heat 2tbs oil in a pan and fry the onions until brown. Mix them with beef, pork and olives by hand. Add the egg white, soy, ketchup and seasoning. On a floured board, roll out cobnut-sized balls. Fry these in the rest of the oil until lightly coloured.

RISSOLES

80g oil • 120g diced onion • 20g dried breadcrumbs
700g minced, beef, lamb pork or a blend • 1 egg
2tbs tomato ketchup • 2tbs Worcester sauce
1 crumbled stock cube • pepper • flour (optional)

Heat 20ml oil in a pan. Fry onions until coloured. Moisten breadcrumbs and squeeze out excess water. Mix onion, bread, mince, egg, ketchup, Worcester sauce and stock cube. Grind plenty of black pepper onto the meat and knead again. Form into rissoles (whatever size you prefer). It's easier on a floured board or with wetted hands. Fry rissoles in the rest of the oil.

MINCE

100ml sunflower oil • 200g diced onions • 2tsp ginger purée
2tsp garlic purée • pinches of powdered cinnamon and clove
1 bayleaf • 3 split green cardamoms
1 tsp chilli pepper or hot paprika • 600g minced beef
200g thick yoghurt • salt

Heat oil in a skillet or *sauteuse* and brown the onions. Mix the ginger and garlic with a little water. Stir in the pan. Add the cinnamon, clove, bayleaf, cardamoms and chilli. Coat with oil. Crumble the mince into the pan. Fry until it starts to colour. Add yoghurt and salt. Turn down the heat. Simmer for 45 minutes, adding a little water if the mince dries out.

HOLY GRAIL

In his earliest, pioneering days when he was still a mere cheesemonger with a shop in Petersfield, Pat Smythe spent a night in our home. He was travelling on the next day to visit a cheese producer outside Lostwithiel. We talked long into the night about his ambition to make his own, one that would rival the finest Camembert or Brie. He was passionate, poetic almost, but he didn't light up a room. He never noticed that his listeners had stopped following his arguments, that his personal manifesto wasn't permeating our after-dinner drowsiness. Eventually, he went to bed and he left early the next morning.

Some time later in the day Mary told me, 'Your friend's been wanking all over the sheets.'

This shouldn't have bothered me (it amused her), but I couldn't help making the connection between his nocturnal thrills and my wife – young and pretty then. It seemed somehow to be an abuse of hospitality.

It's probably because I disapproved that I didn't work hard at maintaining a friendship that was based on little more than a shared professional sympathy for cheese. However, I rang him to wish him good luck when I heard (not from him, mind you) that he had bought a smallholding outside Glastonbury where he hoped to make his own cheeses from the flock of Alpine dairy goats he had installed.

Pat wasn't obsessive in any clinical sense of the word, but he directed all his energy and his money to achieve his goal.

After he had sold his shop to pay for the move to the Somerset Levels, he had no money left over. At first there was little or no income either. He expected his wife to buy clothes for herself and the children from jumble sales. In winter, they couldn't afford to switch on the central heating. Their lifestyle could have passed for alternative, except that they were a Home Counties couple with neither hippy tendencies nor any middle-class idealistic baggage.

What mattered was the cheese. With his first attempts he successfully produced fresh curds like the cottage cheeses our great-grannies used to make by tying curdled milk in muslin bags and hanging them to dry. From there he graduated to little white discs, hockey pucks that hardened to a feisty, concentrated flavour that seemed to catch fire in the back of the mouth. These, he later claimed, were his summer fantasies, his apprenticeship. They helped to start paying the bills, but they were only a stepping stone.

His aim was to produce a winter cheese similar to the famous Franco-Swiss Vacherin Mont d'Or which is so silky, so slippery it has to be scooped with a spoon. He'd discovered somewhere (how I don't know because he couldn't read French) that it had originally been made from goat's rather than cow's milk. What he thought the damp, flat water meadows of England had in common with frozen alpine pastures, only he knew, but through sheer doggedness, in his third year, he succeeded in developing an unique cheese that he had the wit to christen Holy Grail.

He did all the right things to attract the media's attention. He packed it in a handmade rush box. In the archives at Bridgwater Library, he said, he had discovered references to an eighteenth-century slipcoated goat's cheese that had helped to solve the ripening problem that had been baffling him. He interviewed well. Properly edited, his sincerity, his intensity and his knowledge made for excellent television.

An alert producer snapped him up to present an eight-part prime-time series, *Say Cheese*, in which he visited other artisans, stroked their cows, milked their ewes and pressed, poked or probed ageing wheels in mouldy cellars. Naturally, there was a bestseller, launched for the Christmas market, to accompany it. Fortnum and Mason's hired him to front their Tribute to Territorials, 'Eight centuries of hard cheese'.

When we spoke, which we still did perhaps twice a year, he shrugged off the fame that had come his way, insisting that what mattered to him was that people enjoyed his cheese, that he sold everything he made. Yes, it was nice to be able to afford a new Land Rover. Yes, it was nice that Kitty, his wife, didn't have to complain about having no housekeeping.

What really chuffed him though was the response the Italians had accorded him when he had taken Holy Grail to the Slow Food movement's annual knees-up in Bra. They had treated him like a demi-god. Recognition by his peers ('They feel for cheese') mattered to him.

Listeriosis is one of those intermittently newsworthy food-born diseases. Someone who catches it may suffer flu-like symptoms that they would not probably think of linking to what they had eaten. Pregnant women, though, risk losing the baby they are carrying, which is why it's the ideal ground on which the health police, which wants all we eat to be thermized, sterilized, pasteurized or ionized, fight their battles.

They can say incontrovertibly that pregnant women who eat soft cheese made from raw milk are at risk of losing their babies. The fact that women since the time of Eve have given birth without the benefits of *heat treatment* to protect them doesn't concern them. They argue that in a civilized world no mother-to-be should endure the risk of accidentally or mistakenly swallowing Stilton or Camembert that threatens the life of the unborn.

'No we aren't spoil-sports,' they protest. 'Cheese makers can do what they've always done, providing that they kill all the nasty bugs their milk contains first. If they also have to destroy the nice bugs that make the taste special, unique, an enriching experience, something that brings tears of pleasure to the eye, well that's a small price to pay.'

Here I'm paraphrasing Pat's ironic point of view, because I'm a committed conformist myself, who prefers to hang on to my farm, my dairy and my family rather than cross swords with Environmental Health or the Tesco buyer who pays for my holidays to Provence – where I don't have to worry about making compromises to make a living.

When the story that an unmarried teenage mother-to-be had

suffered a miscarriage after eating Holy Grail broke, the scene was set for one those 'Let's get...' scenarios that are the contemporary, approved alternative to blood sports. It was the alert press officer at an improving hospital who tipped off the *Mail*. She was astute enough to give the national title an exclusive before sending out the release, ensuring that every news station within an hour's drive would send a crew to the hospital to report the story.

The manager of the local health authority immediately shut down Pat's dairy, blocking all sales and impounding all his stock. A thoroughly efficient person with an eye to the future, he would have ordered the goats to be humanely shot but his power didn't extend quite that far.

Pat didn't do himself any favours by standing up in front of the cameras to condemn everyone, from the medical profession to the press, for picking on him. He knew as much or more about the listeria bacteria as anyone, he said. Rather than switch to producing a pasteurized cheese he'd be buggered by a billy.

Of course he was getting ahead of himself, because he wasn't making any cheese at all. The men in white overalls had visited his dairy and taken samples from every nook, every cranny, any possible or improbable breeding ground, for the killer bug. They condemned out of hand what stocks he was keeping, even when they failed to find any traces of the bacteria in the Holy Grail.

'Whether they find anything or not isn't the point,' he complained to me (he had called me out of the blue when I was about to fall asleep). 'They want my head on a stick, so they can wave it around, so that every dairy that still works with raw milk will switch to pasteurization. They don't tell the public that they're more at risk of catching listeriosis from a hot dog or a slice of turkey pumped full of polyphosphates and God knows what other poisonous substances than from my cheese.'

The story had gone cold before the health Gestapo traced the source of the infection. Ironically, Pat was proved right. The owner of a Harrogate deli to which he'd posted a small consignment had cross-contaminated the cheese by handling it after he'd picked at some infected Belgian pâté.

At this point, the story should have a happy ending. In the real world things don't always pan out as they do in the fairy tales. The production company that had planned a follow-up to *Say Cheese* cancelled: 'We don't think the time is right for another series. Maybe next year.'

The supermarket buyer who had been far and away his best customer rang him: 'Great news about you having the all-clear. We should love to start taking Holy Grail again, but of course you would have to switch to pasteurization. Yes, we realize that you weren't to blame, but it's about public perception. Once a reporter tells 15 million viewers on the *Nine O'clock News* that your unpasteurized goats' cheese killed a teenager's baby, that's what sticks in the mind. You can't blame them. You certainly can't blame us.'

Pat says he hung up at that point, stamped from his office to the kitchen and had a row with his wife, not their first. They usually ended with her charging him, 'Haven't I stood by you?'

She never quite managed, 'The children will starve.' That though wasn't too far off the mark, because he had expanded his flock during the heady days of his celebrity. He'd never been a particularly effective money manager, he had lost two months' cash flow, his best customer had pulled the plug, the small specialist shops owned, he always thought, by enthusiasts like himself couldn't take the risk of buying what they might not be able to sell, the fancy restaurants that displayed Holy Grail in the middle of their cheese boards found something to replace it and he was mentally exhausted.

Before he went broke, as he was bound to, Mrs Smythe had the sense to file for a divorce which guaranteed that the farm would have to be sold and she would, at least, recuperate something from a marriage that had become hateful to her.

Pat had spoken to me when he knew that his farm, his business and his precious cheese were lost. He probably contacted me as a last resort. Would I be interested in buying his flock? Goats weren't my thing, I told him. He knew I was an ewe person and what did they say about sheep and goats not mixing?

I felt sorry for him, there but for the grace of Allah the all Merciful and all that, so without thinking I invited him to come and spend a weekend with us, take some time out. Surprisingly, he agreed.

The man who showed up on a Friday evening wasn't the misunderstood genius broken by an unsympathetic society that I'd half expected, nor even a contemporary Job, rolling with the punches of a bullying God. He was uncannily unchanged. The fury he directed against his perceived enemies was in character. So was his reasoned acceptance of his wife's escape: 'Looked at from her perspective, it's probably the right thing to do. Living with me hasn't ever been easy.'

What was he planning on doing next, my wife asked. She had waited until Sunday lunch before broaching the subject, a late after-the-pub affair, our stomachs already sloshing about with Real Ale.

'The obvious thing would be to roll over, give in, but that's not me, is it?'

'So?' my wife persisted.

'So perhaps I'll go out with a bang. Then I'll start again, find something else. Maybe I'll woo my wife or stalk her if she won't have me back, maybe teach myself to become a proper father. Can't be any harder than making cheese. It might turn out more rewarding.'

The meal over, we went out into the afternoon sunshine, slept off some of the booze, walked the dogs. For me it was a perfect day, what I worked for. That was the difference between Pat and me. I worked so I could enjoy a beer, a stroll down a country lane, whatever. The adjoining compartment that was my farm had a connecting door but I kept it separate. He, well, he never left his private study. No, that won't do. He was, like, always on his own planet.

When he had left, I gave Mary a hug, partly to thank her, partly in relief.

'Could have gone worse,' she said.

'Actually, I thought he was surprisingly in control.'

We had one of those telepathic moments that couples who have lived happily together have every so often. 'Do you think he left his visiting card, like the last time he stayed?' I asked.

'Not that I noticed,' Mary replied. ' I stripped the bed as soon as he'd gone, aired his room.'

'Good!' I wasn't sure what I meant though.

Pat drove straight back to his farm. Early next morning he went out into the field where his goats were grazing. He took a shotgun with him. Systematically, he began killing them one by one. When he had used up the cartridges he had, he drove into town to buy more, returned and finished the job.

Methodical, he rang the RSPCA to warn them of what he had done in case, he obligingly said, they had to gather evidence for the prosecution that he expected would follow.

I was the next person to learn about the crime. He was reassuring. 'Don't worry, I'm not going to do anything silly.'

He didn't. Instead he entrusted himself to a clutch of psychiatrists and counsellors before doing what he had hinted to us. He went back to his wife. They run a village post office.

toasted cheese

'Chapter 5, Sixty-five Sizzling Rabbits'. They don't write cookery books like they used to.

It was about toasted cheese. 'Recipes for Blushing Bunny', 'Rum Tum Tiddy' and 'Pink Poodle' bubbled off the pages. More cocktail than cookery, a stringy-cheese procession of variations on a theme. Had the author tested every recipe? Unlikely. Did they all work? Possibly. What stitched them together was the author's drooling erudition.* He veered from quotations from nineteenth-century poems published in *Punch* to the Welsh Lady Llanover's cookery book, from Dr Johnson at Ye Olde Cheshire Cheese to a letter from Charles Lamb to Samuel Taylor Coleridge, author of *The Ancient Mariner*.

As enthusiastic on the printed page as the personality-projector on the flat screen, he rattled off tips for chafing dishes, advice on toast (toasted one side and which way up, buttered how, soaked in ale, with or without crusts) and the two basic methods for this dish: one with milk and the other with beer.

The details and asides – 'a boiled rabbit is a spoiled rabbit' – compensated for directions to stir the cheese in one direction only for upwards of 10 minutes 'to keep it from curdling, getting stringy or rubbery.' In that time, our contemporary artistes would expect to have a three-course banquet on the table with their guests tucking into the dessert.

* Bob Brown, *The Complete Book of Cheese*, with an introduction by Clifton Fadiman and illustrations by Eric Blegvad, Gramercy Publishing Co., New York, 1955.

Tucked among the literary and culinary scavenging was a rarebit attributed to an Irish essayist Dr William Maginn: 'I like it best in the genuine Welsh way, however – that is, the toasted bread buttered on both sides profusely, then a layer of cold roast beef with mustard and horseradish, and then, on the top of all, the superstratum, of Cheshire *thoroughly* saturated, while in the process of toasting, with genuine porter, black pepper, and shallot vinegar.'

However unlikely it may be that anyone will ever attempt to produce this (and setting aside the fact that it had little to do with Wales), there's no doubt about its charm and the context adds to the piquancy: butter made from unpasteurized cream freshly churned, bread not out of a packet, roast beef with an overcoat of fat crisp from the spit, hot made-mustard, grated horseradish, cloth-bound Cheshire cheese, dark-and-malty beer and finely minced shallots steeped in vinegar. Every ingredient suggests patience, care and skill… even though the end product, to me, seems greasy and indigestible.

It's perhaps churlish to have written about a chapter of a cookery book which is probably out of print without giving its title, but it stands for the waifs and strays gathering dust in the backrooms of libraries or on collectors' shelves. Nobody would publish them now; their nearest equivalents are blogs (although, that said, Bob Brown's book is available in a more recent edition).

At the bottom of the basic Welsh rabbit recipe its author advised, 'Give a thought to the sad case of the "little dog whose name was Rover, and when he was dead he was dead all over." Something very similar happens with a Rabbit that's allowed to cool down – when it's cold it's cold all over, and you can't resuscitate it by heating.' Think of cold mozzarella on a half-eaten pizza and the image comes to life.

It also holds true for the current flush of literature and television features. Dished up fresh and piping hot, they're as appetizing as Pink Poodle (cheese blended with California claret and cream of tomato soup). Set aside for a while, they lose their savour. History remembers Fanny Cradock for her angry, shrivelled, bony face glaring in black and white through a cathode ray tube – just, but not for anything she cooked.

TOASTED MONTGOMERY'S CHEDDAR

1 thick slice sourdough bread • 10g butter
2–3 sprigs land cress or watercress • Worcester sauce
40g grated Montgomery's Cheddar

Toast the bread. Let it cool a little. Spread with butter. Put the cress on next. Press the cheese over the toast. Melt it under the grill. Splash Worcester sauce on top.

PEAR AND PARMESAN RABBIT

20g butter • 40g grated Parmesan • 2tbs perry or dry cider
1 egg yolk • black pepper • 1 slice sourdough bread
1 ripe conference pear

Stand a bowl over pan of boiling water. Melt half the butter in it. Add the cheese and stir until pasty. Beat perry, egg and pepper. Whisk into the cheese until it melts. Take off the heat and continue whisking. Toast the bread and butter it. Cover with slices of pear. Spoon cheese mixture on top and glaze under the grill.

CHEESE AND TOMATO CROQUE MONSIEUR

4 thin slices sourdough bread • 30g butter
2–3 rashers bacon • 1 sliced tomato
pepper • 40g grated Cheddar

Cut the bread to sandwich-toaster size. Butter and reserve. Fry the bacon until it starts to crisp. Add the tomato and cook to a mush. Season with pepper. Lay out two of your slices of bread (buttered sides down) and cover with the bacon and tomato. Press the grated cheese on top. Make two sandwiches by topping off with the other two slices, buttered sides uppermost. Toast in a sandwich-toaster until crisp and golden.

purée

Joël Robuchon, not long ago the most famous chef in the world, built his reputation around one dish, potato purée – mash. He did it by going over the top and then a bit further. To a kilo of potatoes weighed before peeling, he added 500 grams of butter after boiling. By beating the two together he created an unctuous emulsion that broke every dietary law. Excess and luxury stuck two fingers up to judgement and common sense.

His signature dish popped up at the tail end of the Nouvelle Cuisine fad. It was an era of fruit *coulis* (purées passing themselves off as sauces) and mousses (purées compacted with egg white and cream). Once the gastronomic press twigged that *haute cuisine* was baby food in disguise, it turned snippy and the whole edifice collapsed.

Chef Robuchon's butter-and-Belle-de-Fontenay did one thing right. It matched supply and demand. His customers at Jamin in Paris's 16e weren't hungry with the appetite of navvies when they sat down to dine. They were avid for surprises and sensations. He delivered. A perfectly formed quenelle that melted in their mouth matched their expectations to perfection.

In a home, mash has to meet a more exacting standard. If it deviates from the routine – too dry, too sloppy, too salty, not salty enough, too rich, too bland, too peppery, or lumpy – somebody will notice. The best one can hope for is that it gets eaten without comment. No matter that it would be nice to switch the butter for olive oil once in a while or perk it up with celeriac or some grated cheese. Such refinements, all legitimate for the creative cook, are off-limits to his or her identical twin trying to make his or her skills invisible.

The flip side of this is that nobody can say such and such a recipe is right: each to his own, and there are probably more variants than even a creative maestro like Monsieur Robuchon could think of. What does he, for instance, know about the differences between Desirée and King Edwards, or the taste of a potato that has been microwaved in its skin then peeled?

Although the definitive mash recipe can't exist, there are tips of the granny-knows-best kind that help. One, so obvious it's almost too embarrassing to mention, is to boil similar-sized chunks. So is putting them into cold salted water (10g of salt per litre as a rule of thumb) and bringing it up to the boil. Another is not to overcook them. A third is to drain them well and, where possible, dry them out a bit before mashing. Steamed potatoes tend to be stickier, boiled fluffier. Mealy ones, baked in their skins, are more earthy.

Bashing them and forcing them through a ricer are two means to the same end. One is better if there are going to be left-overs, planned for bubble-and-squeak or fish cakes where the odd lumps are a bonus; the other suits a smoother, silkier purée, the kind that is beaten with a wooden spoon.

HADDOCK AND CELERIAC FISH PIE

500g peeled and chopped potato • salt
250g peeled and diced celeriac • 700g smoked haddock fillets
600ml milk • 120g butter • 60g flour
pepper • 100g chopped spring onions

Boil potatoes in a pan of salted water. Boil celeriac in another. Poach or microwave haddock in 500ml milk until cooked. Skin and break the fish into chunks. Put in an ovenproof dish. Make a roux with 60g butter and the flour. Whisk in the milk. Stir until it thickens. Simmer 15 minutes. Pour over the fish. Purée the potato and celeriac. Add milk, butter, pepper and spring onions. Spoon over the fish. Bake in a hot oven until the top browns (25 minutes).

CAULIFLOWER MASH

500g peeled potatoes • salt • 150g trimmed cauliflower
2tbs milk • 80g butter • pepper

Cook the potatoes in boiling salted water. Cook the cauliflower in boiling salted water until very soft. Use a ricer to purée potatoes and cauliflower. Heat the milk and butter in a pan. Add the vegetables. Beat until creamy. Season with pepper.

CRUSHED POTATOES, BACON, FRIED ONION AND KALE

700g peeled potatoes • salt • 30ml sunflower oil
120g diced streaky bacon • 120g sliced onion
300g curly kale • 50ml milk • black pepper

Roughly chop the potatoes and boil in salted water. Heat the oil in a frying-pan and fry the bacon and onion. Roughly chop the kale and boil in salted water. Drain as soon as it's tender. Drain the potatoes. Put them back in the saucepan with milk and crush them, leaving some lumps. Season with pepper and fold in the other ingredients.

LEEK WITH LEEK

2–3 chunky leeks, about 600g • salt • 500g peeled potatoes
80ml double cream • 50g butter • pepper
1tbs oil • 100g diced streaky bacon

Discard the green tops leaving about 15cm of green attached. Cut the white into rings about 4cm thick. Chop the green leaves. Boil the whites in plenty of salted water and drain. Reserve. Boil the roughly chopped potatoes in the same water. Add the chopped green leek towards the end of cooking. Drain the potato and leek. Mash with cream, butter and pepper. Heat the oil in a pan and fry streaky bacon until crisp. Add the leek white, long enough to heat through. Serve the white leek and bacon on the creamed leek mash.

charlottes

…potatoes, not the creamy desserts swaddled in boudoir biscuits.

We used to grow another variety, Belle de Fontenay, that was so popular with a colony of small slugs on our plot, we had to switch. Our neighbours fill their sacks with impressive maincrop spuds. By comparison our Charlottes look like failures, a large one may weigh a few ounces and the smallest ones, no bigger than a child's marbles, almost nothing.

So why do we persist? It has something to do with national culture. Bintje, the Low Countries favourite, suits the Belgian passion for crisp French fries. In Britain, Maris Pipers fuel our fish and chip shops and there may be an unconscious folk memory that larger potatoes equate with less spud bashing. In France, where the family tree of *pommes sautées* has a dozen branches and countless scions, smaller and firmer potatoes have more appeal.

If we want bog-standard Brit-pot we can buy it at the farm gate. For sautéing we'll fall back on our own resources. This means in effect that our Charlottes are seasonal in the much the same way that new potatoes are. We watch the haulms flowering and withering. We guess which one to dig up first. We notice how their taste and texture alters. We'll tackle the larger ones first, leaving the chats (the baby ones that were once fed to the pigs) until last. And, in their own way, shrivelled and dry, they're a treat in their own right.

Serious folk who know have a scale for measuring potatoes. At one end is 'waxy' and at the other 'floury'. In practical terms, those that are mealy can fall apart when they're boiled too long. Waxy Charlottes keep their shape, at least they will unless they're cooked to perdition.

Without tackling the whole repertoire of sauté recipes, it's worth breaking them into two groups. In Method A they're shallow-fried from raw; in Method B they're boiled or steamed before frying. Within these parameters it's possible to tinker endlessly: skin on, skin off; sliced thin, cubed, in wedges; fried crisp, gooey; with lard, butter, oil or any combination of these; with or without garlic, fried onions, bacon, herbs.

Beyond ingredients, it's also about controlling the heat: turning the flame up or down, or covering the pan at first so the potatoes steam while they fry, or tossing them in the pan – the original, literal sense of *sauter*. This has less to do with planning: 'Today, my Charlottes shall be uniformly irregularly browned in the style of my mother-in-law', and more to do with reaction, recognizing what's going on in the pan and working with it.

The outcome isn't or shouldn't be something to crow about. It's a potato, something you eat with a fried egg. Pretending to be savant and knowledgeable about the flavour is silly. It may have its place in a specialist laboratory, not at the supper table.

This is a description of a Charlotte from an authoritative source: 'In the mouth it is full-bodied, and tastes equally fresh and buttery, with a lingering note of sweetness. The flavour is remarkably long and persistent. The texture is firm to bite, but it gives way immediately to a supple, velvety melting quality.' Penned by a Master of Wine, it's most likely true in every detail, but I could never enjoy ours half so much if I were to deconstruct them in that way.

SAUTÉED CHATS AND BACON

500g Charlotte chats • 120g streaky bacon
50ml sunflower oil

Boil the chats in their skins 10 minutes. Drain, refresh and peel them. Cut the bacon into small pieces. Heat the oil in a large frying-pan. Sauté the potatoes in oil. Keep turning and add bacon when they start colouring. Continue to sauté until the bacon is crisp.

SAUTÉED CHARLOTTES AND CEPS

500g peeled Charlottes • salt • 400g ceps
60ml oil • 60g butter • 2 crushed garlic cloves
chopped parsley • pepper

Parboil the potatoes 10 minutes in salted water. Drain and cut into
thick slices. Cut out the spongy undersides of the ceps and discard
them. Slice the ceps and fry them in 50ml oil. When they leech juice
strain it off. Set the ceps to one side. Heat the butter and oil in a large
frying-pan. Sauté the potatoes until they brown. Add the ceps and
garlic. Fry for a couple of minutes. Stir in parsley and season.

CARAMELIZED CHARLOTTES

500g small whole Charlottes • 60g sunflower oil • 30g butter
10g caster sugar • salt • chopped parsley

Parboil the potatoes in their skins five minutes. Drain and peel. Heat
the oil in a skillet or frying-pan. Add the potatoes and cook over a
medium heat until they colour. Discard the oil in the pan. Replace
with the butter. Sprinkle sugar on the potatoes. Turn up the heat.
Shake the pan to help the potatoes caramelize a little. Finish with a
little salt and chopped parsley.

POTATO AND GREEN BEAN SALAD

500g boiled Charlottes • 250g boiled *haricots verts*
1 large gherkin • 100g smoked salmon • 3tbs mayonnaise
1tbs tomato ketchup • 1tsp Worcester sauce • black pepper

Wait until the potatoes cool and chop them into hazelnut sized pieces. Halve the beans if they are on the large side. Dice the gherkin. Cut the smoked salmon in thin strips. Combine mayonnaise, ketchup and Worcester sauce. Mix ingredients together and grind black pepper on them.

field mushrooms and other edible fungi

Fungal snobbery is unpleasant. It can turn chance encounters with edible wild mushrooms into a tasteless game of status-seeking where the nibbling classes go into raptures over puffballs they've known or the copse where they found a cluster of chanterelles.

Our experience has been random, intermittent and non-specific. We may visit a field three days running if we happen on a flush of field mushrooms. Alternatively, we may spend a year without foraging for any kind of fungus. One year we may harvest the gelatinous Jew's Ears sticking out from an overhanging branch. They'll go well in a stir-fry. Another, we'll ignore them.

Because we know a wood where ceps grow, we won't drive the seven miles necessary to forage for them – and for a good reason. Fungus is capricious. It doesn't come up in the same spot, at the same time each year, or in the same abundance. Even if it does, assorted insects are likely to have first pickings. By the time a large *boletus* mushroom has flattened to its full extent, it will be riddled with worms. By the time its spongy underbelly has been cut out, there will be very little left worth eating.

That said, over the years and without any special expertise, we've learnt not so much the basics of mycology, but how to extract something worthwhile from the fungus that we do bring home. Just as an old-fashioned French gourmet knows that his fresh truffle should be eaten as soon as possible and that it will be better in an omelette than as a slice on top of a fillet steak, so we've discovered, by trial and error, what works for us in our kitchen. We are justifiably thrilled if we happen upon a cache of wood blewits – it doesn't happen every year – because we know that even a few will be a serious treat if we fry them for a few seconds in butter.

Field mushrooms aren't all alike. They can be gorged with water or dry, small and plump or blowsy. In the pan, they can wilt to little more than a dark, flabby mess, but the same 'mess' can form the basis of a black, scary soup that's actually delicious, quite unlike the speckled textbook soups most rustic cooks aim for.

By the same token it would be a shame to turn chunky horse mushrooms into a soup. A large one sautéed, perhaps with a little garlic, a squeeze of lemon juice and some some chopped parsley is a recipe that is hard to better. Piling slices, seared for a few moments until they colour, on toast with a splash of Lea & Perrins so that the cooking juices and ketchup seep into the buttered bread, matches it.

There's one secret about all edible fungi that is worth sharing: they rarely make good garnishes. Their nutritional value boils down to very little. Reducing what's already negligible to something less is silly. For all their designer charms they're food for enjoying on their own terms, for their shapes, their colour and above all their taste. Combine them with other ingredients by all means, but as an add-on they're wasted.

NOTES ON WILD MUSHROOMS AND FUNGI I'VE TRIED AND LIKED:*

Agaricus macrosporus – hefty mushroom, firm and chunky. Very good.

Amethyst Deceiver – pretty colour (though this can vary), bit soft and mild taste.

Bay Boletus – related to ceps (q.v.) and good for soup or flavouring as well as for omelettes and the rest.

Beefsteak Fungus – red like raw pickled ox-tongue (appearance isn't dissimilar either), it sheds masses of starchy juice when fried. Throw this out and start again and the fungus is quite meaty with a hint of citrus flavour.

Cauliflower Fungus – it's more like a giant, colourless carnation and it tastes nothing like its name suggests. A single example can weigh over a kilo (several meals) but it doesn't have an especially characteristic taste.

Cep – their English name Penny Bun hints at the size and shape when they're fully grown. I prefer them when they're closed like a boxing glove on the end of a muscular forearm. The pores under the cap on mature fungi are better cut out before cooking.

Chanterelle – beloved of chefs. I find that they're nicer to eat if they're dry-fried to extract excess moisture and then re-fried in hot butter.

Chicken of the Woods – its name describes the texture (factory-farm chicken) but it has a pleasant mild taste.

Clytocybe geotropa – firm and quite meaty, a medium-large frying mushroom, similar to funnel caps (q.v.).

Common Funnel Cap – firm, meaty and tasty.

Common White Helvella – related to morels (q.v.) but a poor relation.

Common Yellow Russula – edible member of a large group of fungi; it's brittle and, though common, often eaten by slugs before humans.

Fairy Ring Champignon – what the French call *mousserons* (from which our mushroom); strong mushroom taste and a fair amount of bite.

Field Mushroom – closely related to cultivated mushrooms, their flavour varies according to their age and also where they grow.

Giant Puffball – I've picked them weighing over three kilos. After eating them for two or three days, they're quite bland really. I've ended up chucking out a large chunk.

Horn of Plenty (Fr. *Trompette de la Mort*) charcoal fungus similar in taste and appearance to chanterelles (q.v.).

Hedgehog Fungus – often added as a garnish to pretty plated food and it tastes quite strong.

Horse Mushroom – similar to *Agaricus macrosporus*, large and long-stemmed.

Jew's Ear – politically incorrect term for rubbery fungus that's popular in Chinese cuisine partly because of its texture and partly because it absorbs other flavours.

Leucopaxillus giganteus – large white toadstool; good texture but quite bland.

Parasol Mushroom – large and flat capped; good grilled with butter and then hazelnut oil and salt.

Morels – delicious honeycombed mushroom that grows in the spring; best with sherry-cream reduction sauce. There are several varieties, all potent and all better than the dried version that is sometimes sold by posh delis.

Oak Milk Cap – one expert says they smell 'oily or suggesting bugs'. I've not noticed. Good in stews.

Oyster Mushrooms – the wild fungi that grow on dead logs are tasty but the cultivated version is bland.

Pleurotus cornucopia – cousin of the oyster mushroom (q.v.), it grows in clumps on dead wood, pale beige and good eating, a bit gritty.

Puffballs – small puffballs when they're fresh are a better bet than the giant ones, but still on the bland side.

Saffron Milk Cap – member of the *Lactarius* family (brittle, and white sap comes out when broken); really good flavour (I've only eaten this in France).

Scarlet Elf Cap – pretty little bright red fungus that grows on dead wood. Useful to brighten up a dish and the light mushroom taste is pleasant.

Shaggy Ink Cap – they look like whiteish fluffy gherkins when young. Cooked they melt away to nothing but they form the base for a very good mushroom ketchup.

Shaggy Parasol – similar to the parasol; some people have an allergic reaction, not me.

St George's Mushroom – rare, but a treat in spring when not many mushrooms are about.

Summer Truffle – freshly harvested this is very tasty, but it's not to be confused with the intense fragrance of a Périgord truffle (*Tuber melanosporum*) that doesn't grow in Britain.

The Blusher – easy to confuse with the poisonous Panther Cap (can be riddled with parasitic worms) – makes good soup.

The Charcoal Burner – another edible *Russula* with a greyish top and white underbelly; brittle but a good mushroom taste.

The Miller – its name indicates the flavour; bit like a white chanterelle to look at.

The Prince – really well-flavoured mushroom, it grows in woods rather than open meadows.

Wood Blewit – lilac gills, pale brown slightly waxy top. One of the best wild fungi around: firm textured, bags of taste (field blewits are said to be equally good, but I've never come across them).

...and one I shouldn't have tried

Yellow Stainer – it looks like a field mushroom and grows in meadows, but when you rub the cap it leaves a dirty yellow stain. The effect? It kept me glued to a lavatory seat for several hours, gradually dehydrated, but I was spared the cramps, sweating and flushes they are said to cause.

Mushrooms by Roger Phillips (Pan) is the best book around for wannabe foragers; and, whatever you do, make sure you know what you're eating.

DRYING MUSHROOMS

Anywhere dry and warm works. Time will vary from a few hours to a day. Slice ceps or other bulbous ones. Lay the mushrooms in a single layer on a tray. Dry until crisp or they may spoil. Keep in airtight jars.

DUXELLES FOR FLAVOURING

1 kilo mushrooms, ceps, etc. • 300g shallots or onions
60g butter or oil

Dice the mushrooms or ceps until they look like grit. Finely dice the shallots or onions. Melt the butter in a large pan. Add the shallots/onions and sweat until transparent. Stir in the mushrooms/ceps. Stew over a low heat until most of the moisture evaporates. Freeze in 10 small packets or an ice-cube tray. Add a cube to soups, sauces, stuffings or stews.

GRILLED PUFFBALL STEAKS

600g freshly picked puffball • 40g melted butter
salt and pepper • 50ml hazelnut oil

Cut four 150g steaks (about 2cm thick) off a puffball. Brush one side with melted butter and grill buttered side up. When brown, turn, brush and grill the other side. Season and brush with hazelnut oil. Eat very hot.

FIELD MUSHROOM SOUP

50g butter • 200g diced onion • 200g diced potato
1 diced stick of celery • 400g chopped field mushrooms
2 chicken stock cubes • 500ml water • 500ml milk
salt and pepper

Melt the butter in a large saucepan. Sweat the onions until transparent. Add onion, potato, celery and mushrooms. Stir until the mushrooms collapse and blacken. Crumble the stock cube in boiling water. Pour into the pan. Add the milk. Simmer 10–15 minutes. Liquidize the soup and season it.

unscrambled eggs

Here's a sketch for a scrambled egg recipe:

'Melt a large knob of butter in a pan with a little salt and pepper. Add six beaten eggs and stir over a very low heat until soft curds form. Serve on buttered toast.'

Puff up the details, *Ulysses*-style, and the words could stretch to several pages: what kind of pan, what sort of butter, salt, pepper, exactly how much; what kind of eggs, what size, beaten how and for how long, what with; what's a low heat, what should you use for stirring; what precisely are 'soft curds'.

Recipe-junkies chain themselves to sets of instructions. Hobbled, they trudge through a process until they emerge in the sunlight with something palatable that looks almost as good as the picture in the book or on screen.

Cooks are unshackled. They dance in time to the patter of tiny messages scuttling over their sensory organs. What they dish up, good or indifferent, is an extension of who they are, a Bloody Mary of experience and intuition, seasoned with a dash of chance.

Take a step backwards to the business of scrambling. In the mid-twentieth century the French held competitions to choose apprentice Chefs of the Year. The task set to regional finalists was *oeufs brouillés*. In its authentic version it differs from the Anglo-Saxon equivalent. Eggs cook very slowly, very gently, in a double-saucepan until they form an unctuous, creamy mass. The trick is to take the pan off the fire when the texture approaches perfection and beat in a little cold cream or butter. This enriches the eggs while preventing them from overcooking. A fashionable entrée in a grand *établissement* back then might be *oeufs brouillés* served in an eggshell with a Beluga caviar topping.

Contrast these with coagulated lumps, fresh from the cage, that hang about in chafing dishes where hotels regale their guests with a 'Full English' or microwave scrambled eggs, slipping onto the plate like blubber.

Take another step back, from end product to produce. Egg-white is bland. The taste is locked in the yolks. It's a fallacy, though, to match colour with quality. Italian pasteurized egg-yolks are acrylic yellow. In the old Soviet bloc they were sometimes cream-coloured. At a breakfast in Claridge's, I remember them being dirty-traffic-light amber. Nor are egg-shells a pointer to what's inside. Terracotta Welsumers, duck-blue Araucanas or speckled Marans have a seductive appeal. An ex-battery hen, once rehabilitated, doesn't change the shape, size or appearance of her regimented eggs, but their contents will be as good as the pedigree birds'. Diet is the key. What goes in through the beak affects what passes out through the bum.

SCRAMBLED EGGS AND CREAM

6 eggs • salt and pepper
60g butter • 80ml double cream

Beat the eggs and seasonings thoroughly. Melt the butter in a frying-pan. (Keep the heat at its lowest setting.) Add the egg and cook slowly. Keep stirring. Once soft curds have formed, take off the heat. Beat in the cream.

SCRAMBLED EGGS AND SORREL

30g sorrel leaves • 70g butter • 6 eggs
salt and pepper • 2tsp chopped parsley

Remove any tough stalks on the leaves. Chop them as finely as you can. Melt 40g butter in a frying-pan. Keep the heat low. Add the sorrel and stew until it turns khaki. Beat the eggs, salt and pepper. Pour over the sorrel. Scramble the eggs very slowly. Take the pan off the heat when almost done. Incorporate the rest of the butter and parsley.

PIPERADE

50ml olive oil • 250g sliced onion • 150g diced streaky bacon
2 crushed garlic cloves • 400g sliced red peppers
½ tsp pimentón • salt • basil leaves • 4 eggs

Heat the oil in a skillet or *sauteuse*. Add onion and slow-fry until sweet. Add the bacon and garlic. Fry until fragrant. Add the peppers and pimentón. Stew over a low flame until soft. Adjust seasoning and add basil. Beat eggs and pour into the pan. Let them start to set and fold off the bottom. Cook until they are just set but still moist.

PARASOL MUSHROOMS AND SCRAMBLED EGG

2–3 large parasol mushrooms • 50ml sunflower oil
salt • 6 eggs • 50g butter • pepper • 2 slices buttered toast

Discard the mushroom stalks. Roughly chop the caps. Heat the oil in a large pan. Add mushrooms and salt. When cooked they'll shed lots of water. Take the pan off the heat and discard the water and oil. Replace with butter. Turn heat down to low. Beat the eggs with pepper and a little salt. Stir into the pan. Cook very slowly until scrambled. Spoon onto hot buttered toast.

purple sprouting

We've a thick *Encyclopædia of Gardening* published in 1825, containing, it claims, 'All the latest improvements'. It describes, in detail, assorted kinds of sprouting broccoli, both white and purple: 'Sulphur coloured', 'Dwarf', 'Purple Cape' and 'Portsmouth broccoli', varieties 'which will produce beautiful heads in November and continue to do so until Christmas', and one 'whose leaves encompass and compress the head, so as to render it invisible when fit to cut, which is a great preservative from the frosty mornings common in the spring months.' Regency vicars and landed gentry alike craved it and grew it in their sheltered walled gardens the whole year round.

By then, it had been with us for over a century, long enough to have lost its earliest popular name, Italian Asparagus. This, though, gives a clue to how Georgian epicures saw it – something exotic – and how they prepared it, boiled so the florets, like asparagus tips, didn't crumble while the vivid green stalks remained tender.

Modern gardening books say the earliest purple sprouting broccoli flowers in January, a vegetable equivalent of snowdrops. Not *chez nous*. On our little patch they might, when the winter is mild, start coming in dribs and drabs a month later. Picking them is one of those nimble-fingered jobs that take hand–eye co-ordination. True to their name the tender florets sprout willy-nilly from the gnarled cabbage stem. The skill lies in snipping the stems close to the axil, often with a couple of leaves attached so the plant continues to sprout into the spring.

Because it gives us advance warning of winter's end it touches an emotional nerve, but it never receives reverential treatment. We're not going to dish it up as some pukka antipasto. Its place, its natural home, is in a meat-and-two-veg. combo. That's over-egging things because there are times when a plateful, piled high like spaghetti, is, well, supper.

Emptied from a recycled plastic bag onto a work-top, they still need handling with respect. Thicker stalks need splitting so they'll cook at the same rate as thinner ones. Often, in mid-season, it's easier to do a triage, separate the plump from the skinny or sort out all the larger clusters of florets. The effort pays off because these will start crumbling before the stems are ready, not that this is some unforgivable act of culinary barbarism.

Botanists have difficulty telling cauliflowers and sprouting broccoli apart. My answer is that I've never been tempted to douse mine with a cheese sauce. They're supposed to be the same thing as calabrese too, aka broccoli with big butch heads and indestructible stalks. My feeling about these is that a president who rejected them wasn't altogether misguided. Actually, that's a bit unfair on the calabrese. Imported from Italy, it used to provide an ideal hiding place for illegal aliens, caterpillars, but it tasted if not fine, at least edible. They didn't taste bad, the caterpillars that is. It was impossible not to swallow the odd one or two, but they had been boiled.

WARM SPRING GREENS SALAD

500g spring greens • salt • 100ml olive oil
lemon juice to taste • 2tbs stoned black olives

Split or chop any thicker stems on the spring greens. Toss into a litre of boiling salted water. Boil until tender. Drain the greens and squeeze out excess moisture, but reserve 100ml of the water. Put the water, olive oil and a generous tablespoon of greens in a jug. Liquidize and add lemon juice to taste. Toss the greens and olives with the dressing.

PURPLE SPROUTING, LARDONS AND GARLIC CROÛTONS

60ml olive oil • 100g bacon lardons • 2 slices bread
1 clove garlic • 450g purple sprouting broccoli
salt • 1 egg

Heat the oil in a pan and fry the lardons. Fry the bread in the same oil. When it's crisp rub it with garlic and dice into croûtons. Boil roughly chopped broccoli in salted water until tender. Drain and squeeze out excess moisture. Poach the egg in simmering water. Mix lardons, croûtons and greens together. Mash the egg with them. Serve hot.

muttar

It's hard to find anyone with a bad word to say about frozen peas and that's fair enough. Because they are good doesn't mean there's no better. Being picky, their skins are a little leathery; they could be sweeter. Canned French *petits pois*, a drab olive, taste good once one forgets how they started off in life. They don't compete with the real thing.

These are the successful compromises society accepts to enjoy its ration of peas, a vegetable so popular it's boring. The obverse side of this coin is that fresh peas are rare. Eating them is a gardener's privilege, a reward for battles fought with leaf-rollers, weevils, pigeons and mice. He can swap yarns with his peers about the relative merits of Kelvedon Wonders and Hurst Green Shaft or his luck with Douce de Provence.

What he has also learnt by experience is that fresh-picked peas won't wait. The sugars in them start turning to starch within hours. Anyone who has bought 'fresh' peas from a traditional greengrocer only to discover they tasted floury has learnt the hard way how quickly that change occurs.

Perhaps there's a tinge of exaggeration in this picture. A couple of years back, I was in Lucknow. It was February, early spring in north India, in a city whose vegetable markets could compete with anything the Mediterranean has to offer.

Hawkers were doing brisk business with *muttar*, Hindi for peas: pyramids of ravished pods piled to one side of their stalls, half-hiding the brass *handi* they used as cooking pots. For each order, they spooned hot peas in a bowl, mixed them with raw shredded onions, diced tomato, green chilli and spice and dished them up on cardboard plates. It was better than any of the kebabs for which Lucknow is justifiably famous, one of those food memories that don't fade.

The point is the peas were sweet, tender and fresh. They disproved the logical argument for processing raw materials in order to supply urban populations. One of the great Italian recipes, *risi e bisi* from Veneto, not so much a risotto as a pea and rice soup, falls short if it's prepared second-hand, as it were, with a packet of frozen peas. Any decent *nonna* would want to add the fresh pods to the vegetable stock in which she cooked her rice to intensify the flavour.

If ever I were to go down with a Fat Duck virus, I would fill a syringe with melted butter, possibly infused with mint, and inject it through the shells, before steaming or boiling peas. Eating them as finger food would combine the atavistic pleasure of a caveman with post-modern conceptualism.

It isn't going to happen. Instead, there will be *petits pois à la française* with lettuce and spring onions, or peas stewed with bacon lardons and cream maybe. Messing with something so delicious for the sake of creativity doesn't justify itself. I'd rather eat them raw – and I do.

PETITS POIS À LA FRANÇAISE

500g shelled, small peas • salt • 50g shredded lettuce leaves
2 chopped spring onions • 20g softened butter • 15g plain flour

Rain the peas, lettuce and spring onions into boiling water. Simmer until tender. Strain off all the water bar a generous cupful. Crumble the butter and flour together. Bring peas and remaining cooking liquid to the boil again. Whisk in the butter and flour until they thicken the liquid.

PEAPOD SOUP

600ml chicken stock • 400g fresh-picked peapods
a few mint leaves • 200g peas • 100ml double cream • salt

In a largish pan, bring the stock to the boil. Add the peapods and return to the boil. Simmer two minutes. Take off the heat and leave to stand for 20 minutes. Strain the liquid into a clean pan and boil. Add the peas and mint. Simmer until the peas are tender but still green. Add the cream and liquidize. Season with salt.

ANGLO-INDIAN PEAS

100g carrot • salt • 1tsp cumin powder
2cm cinnamon stick • 2tsp honey • lemon juice
1 finely sliced shallot • 350g shelled peas

Shred the carrot. Blanch in boiling salted water for about a minute. Drain most of the water, but leave a splash in the pan. Add the cumin, cinnamon and honey. Boil to a light glaze. Squeeze on lemon juice to taste and mix in the shallot. Boil peas until tender in salted water. Drain and stir into the carrot mixture.

no strings attached

Runner beans 'run' up cane tepee frames. *Les haricots verts* grow in clumps at ground level. To any gardener who has grown climbing varieties of French beans, that's over-simplifying, but let it pass. They belong to the same species. To complicate things, *haricots verts* aren't always green. Deep purple ones change back to green when boiled but the yellow ones, *haricots beurre*, stay yellow even though, blindfolded, it would be quasi-impossible to have the foggiest what colour they were.

Setting aside such befuddling differences, both French beans and flat runner beans are tender in their youth, stringy when old and, yes, I know some varieties have stringiness bred out of them.

Green beans ought to be green. In rural France cooks untainted by Nouvelle Cuisine still boil their *haricots verts* until they turn a military khaki. They taste like worn fatigues too. Even the archimandrite of contemporary haute cuisine, Paul Bocuse, suggested that fifteen minutes bubbling was suitable where ten is plenty, and he was used to *extra fins*, finest of fine beans barely out of their cradles.

At the other extreme, too, many chefs, convinced that *al dente* is Italian for raw, show a few beans the pot, sprinkle them around a plate as a garnish or, worse, tie them into bunches with leek ribbons and drizzle extra virgin olive oil or a butter emulsion over them.

To some extent, runners are spared such indignities. Once upon a time, every household dusted down its Spong in August, fixed it to the kitchen table and one by one (or in pairs) cranked the beans through. Their length and shape dictate that they need slicing or shredding.

This isn't suited to restaurant plates or slates. It's labour intensive too. On top of which it pays, as a preliminary, to pare both edges, starting from the end where they were attached to the vines. Even if nine are tender, the tenth will be fibrous.

Runner bean recipes in the British repertory are nothing if not monotonous: runner beans à la Roast Beef, Yorkshire Pudding and Roast Potatoes; runner beans à la Roast Chicken and New Potatoes; runner beans à la Cod and Chips. In other words they're piled on the plate 'Eat your greens' style. The rest is silence.

In one respect, Mrs Beeton, who only inserted one recipe into her magnum opus of 2000-plus, and all those who have followed her lead were right. There isn't an alternative to boiling. In almost everything else she was wrong. The soda she added to the water destroyed those precious vitamins. Her advice to cook the beans until they sank to the bottom of the saucepan is tantamount to massacre. The kitchen lore she passes on about never covering the pan with a lid, treated as culinary gospel, actually makes no odds.

What does matter is the amount of water. Unless there's plenty and it's boiling hard the temperature drops when the beans go in, they take longer to cook and end up limp, dull and vapid.

RUNNER BEANS AND OAK-SMOKED CHEESE

500g runner beans • salt
100g grated oak-smoked Cheddar

String the beans with a sharp potato peeler. Shred them. Cook them in plenty of boiling water. Drain them and mix with cheese.

HARICOTS VERTS

600g *haricots verts* • salt • 20g flat-leaf parsley
25g butter • 1 crushed clove garlic

Nip the ends of the beans with fingers, scissors or knife. Rain the beans into plenty of boiling salted water. Cook until tender (no raw taste). Chop the parsley, but not to a powder like chefs do. Drain the beans and toss with the other ingredients.

BEAN FETTUCINE

700g runner beans • salt • 300g tomato sauce

String the beans with a sharp potato peeler. Continue slicing them into strips running the length of the beans. Drop them in a pan of boiling salted water and cook until just tender. Drain and toss in hot tomato sauce.

TOMATO SAUCE

600g chopped ripe tomatoes • 2 tomato pedoncules or stalks
125g tomato passata • 2tsp tomato purée
½ chicken stock cube • salt

Put all the tomato ingredients in a pan. Stew very gently 30 minutes. Add stock cube and salt and simmer 10 minutes more. Force the sauce through a chinois or sieve. Splash a little water on the pulp to extract as much sauce as possible. Check seasoning.

fat

Grease is an ugly word. Fat sounds menacing. Weigh them on a set of lexical scales against 'cold pressed extra virgin olive oil' and they both suffer. Cooking without them isn't impossible, but it's impoverished. Before the discovery of nutrition and dietetics, those twin peaks of well-being, nobody questioned how thickly he or she spread the butter.

A northerner who ditches butter for Mediterranean *Olio* is mildly perverse. Potatoes roasted without duck fat or rendered lard are second rate. Anointing a skate wing with a bland rapeseed oil doesn't compensate for *beurre noisette*. Hollandaise with low-fat spread? The mind boggles. Since cooks have spent millennia working with animal grease, it shouldn't be beyond our wits to work with it in a measured way without abandoning it completely.

Butter frying in a pan triggers a Pavlovian reflex akin to the scent of baking bread. It has no alternative. Instead of shunning something that brings so much pleasure on the grounds that it may do harm, the drum that nutritionists like to beat, it's more rational to recognize the thrill of, say, freshly sautéed new potatoes or grilled sole and serve them as a rare treat rather than a routine enjoyment.

The rejected ribbon of fat on a sirloin steak pushed to one side of the plate is a commonplace. Flaps of discarded chicken skin run it a close second. Instead of binning, find a way of using them that works. Removed at the butchery stage, minced up and rendered down, they can, in small doses, lubricate the respective slabs of protein they once protected, adding flavour in a way that their juiciness alone can't manage.

Back in the days of rationing, post-World War II, nobody would have dreamt of wasting bacon fat left over from breakfast. Then it was the ideal medium for frying bubble and squeak. It's as good with *rösti*, even better with an Auvergnat potato pancake, *truffade*.

If fat has received unjust censure, greasy food deserves any sledging directed at it. At the simplest level, a quick dab with a sheet of kitchen paper takes a moment and removes surface tackiness. The problem (it applies as much to oil as to fat) more often has to do with temperature. The soggy chip-shop chips saturating the bag with oil that leeches through to the newspaper isn't the fault of the cooking medium, so much as the inadequate heat which boiled them.

An enduring memory of my childhood is bread and dripping. What made it special? To start with, the fat contained more *beefiness* than the meat. During roasting, the joint's surface caramelized and juices, mingled with melting fat, settled in the bottom of the roasting tin. When they cooled and had set the combined flavours captured the essence of roast beef. It's a lost delicacy because it dates back to a time when the family joint languished in an overheated oven until it was baked through and through. As much shrivelled as roasted, it wasn't an epicurean delight, but the following days' beef dripping mashed up with jellied roast gravy, sprinkled with salt on a crust of white bread – that was something else.

BRAISED CHICKEN DRUMSTICKS

8 chicken drumsticks • 20ml sunflower oil • 150g onions
400g can of tomatoes • 150ml stock • salt
2 pieces dried orange peel • 2 sprigs rosemary
5 crushed garlic cloves • black pepper

Peel the skin off the chicken and chop it small. Render the fat from it with the oil in a frying-pan – the heat low. (Remove the crisp bits for a high-cholesterol snack.) Brown drumsticks in rendered fat and transfer them to a casserole. Brown the onions in the chicken fat. Deglaze the frying-pan with tomato. Pour tomato, onions and stock over chicken. Add salt, orange peel, rosemary and garlic. Cover and simmer 50 minutes. Add black pepper to taste.

KING EDWARDS UNDER THE DUCK

1 kilo King Edwards potatoes • salt • 100g duck fat

Peeling the potatoes is optional. Cut them into slices a centimetre thick. Toss them in salt and melted duck fat. Spread them on a roasting tin large enough to hold them. Stand the duck on a rack above them. Bake in a hottish oven for an hour or so, while the duck roasts. Turn them over if necessary.

DUCK STUFFING

40g duck fat • 120g diced onion • 2 sprigs thyme
½ cup dry bread crumbs • 2tbs duck stock
grated zest ½ lemon • 1–2tbs crumbled sage
salt & pepper • 1 egg

Heat the duck fat in a pan. Fry the onion with the sprigs of thyme until soft. Moisten breadcrumbs with stock. Combine onions, bread, lemon and sage. Season. Lightly beat egg and mix into the stuffing.

POTTED DUCK

1 x 2½ kilo duck • 150g green streaky bacon • 350g pork belly
sprig of sage leaves • sprig of thyme • ½ bayleaf
salt and black pepper

Peel the skin off the duck. Chop it small. Blend it in a food processor with any fat inside the carcase. Cut the legs, wings and breast off the carcase. Cube the bacon and pork belly. Put all the ingredients in a slow-cooker. Simmer for 8 hours. Discard bones and sprigs of herbs. Cut the duck meat into bite-sized chunks. Flake the duck, bacon and belly with a fork. Beat the rendered fat into the meat. Leave to set overnight.

JAM TOMORROW AND
TOMORROW AND TOMORROW

The way down for Jean-Luc dated from his appointment as chef at the Ritz-Carlton Jakarta. The hotel had an intense public relations executive who bedded him, convinced the young man he was destined for greatness and promoted him effectively to the world's gastronomic and travel press. His cuttings book swelled almost as fast as his ego.

'You don't get second chances in this business. This is your moment. Grab it,' was the message his number-one cheerleader repeated over and over: over nightcaps at 4 a.m., between the sheets at 5, and over black coffee at 7. Driven as much by his own will to succeed as by critical reviews or his standing with the hotel's owners who, because they could afford to, lavished gifts upon him, he twisted the screw of pressure to the point when the thread was likely to break.

He was never in any danger of a mental breakdown, his executive skills didn't fail him, but his creative judgement ran out of the youthful enthusiasm that had been stoking it. Ideas still flowed from his inventive brain, but they were tired or silly or half-baked.

Nobody noticed, of course. The limelight initially protects those in it with a glamour that puts them beyond criticism.

It wasn't long though before he realized that the part of his work that he had enjoyed the most was turning into a chore he dreaded. He'd sit in his office with a glass of champagne, flicking through cookery books that used to trigger his imagination, hoping to discover ideas that refused to surface. The level of wine in the bottle would sink. His notepad would fill with sketches of cauliflowers, artichokes, large breasts and chaotic, doodled shapes. In the end, faced with the necessity of an executive decision, he would lift a whole menu from some budding Australian or American talent, changing a few garnishes to disguise the provenance.

Customers may not have noticed his gentle decline but his sous-chefs did. Attracted to him, even seeking him out while he had been at his peak, they packed their bags, added his name to their CVs and moved on once they realized he had nothing new to teach them. In their shoes, he thought, he would have done the same thing. Perhaps, he argued with himself, he should return to Europe, maybe open his own restaurant where he could rekindle the energy that had hauled him so quickly to the top of his profession.

To do this meant severing his personal ties. His 'She', he half-understood, was half-hoping to marry him. It would, theoretically, be a pragmatic union. At a deeper level, though, he blamed her in part, probably more than she deserved, for wearing him down. If she hadn't continually pushed the media down his gullet like some *foie gras* duck, he might have become another Escoffier, a Gagnaire. Without her, he might still.

So, in the interests of glory, his career and his craft he threw his girlfriend overboard, handed in his notice and headed back to Europe, consoling himself with the thought that every genius needs at least one failure before he can fulfil himself. In any event he hadn't failed; he was returning with an international reputation.

A sleeping-partner, a place with his own name above the door in his home-town of Cannes, a sunburst of attention, of public excitement during his opening, a honeymoon period with Gault & Millau, even a flush of inventiveness when he adapted tricks he had picked up in south-east Asia to the Côte d'Azur kept him buoyed up and happy, not that he had much time to examine his personal feelings. He didn't sleep much, didn't need to. Whenever fatigue crept up on him, he easily found something chemical or alcoholic to keep him going.

What destroyed him in the long term was the off-season, days when nobody showed up for lunch, nights when he had more wage bills to pay than bums on seats. He found himself in a catch-22 situation where he couldn't stop haemorrhaging cash, but where it would have cost him more to shut down for the winter.

At the end of his third year, after a New Year's Eve gala, he closed ostensibly for redecorations; in fact to shut up shop for good.

'Tough shit,' he mused, before going to work in a nineteenth-century copy of a Loire Valley château, a hotel that did a roaring trade with middle-aged Parisians entertaining their mistresses. It turned out to be a perfect position for cutting the throat of any latent ambition he had to be one of the great names of his generation. He earned a Michelin star in his second year, which kept the owners off his back. They were more interested in filling the four-poster beds and selling bottles of Dom Perignon, Louise and the Veuve anyway.

The ready access to good champagne did wonders for Jean-Luc's thirst. He'd always enjoyed the taste. Nor was he averse to its stimulating effect. If he'd drunk a bottle before lunch, it didn't prevent him doing his job. Nobody knew except for the sommelier who connived with the disappearance of stock, most of which had arrived as backhanders and samples from the wine reps in exchange for an occasional lobster, maybe a couple of soles to take back home, a nice piece of Beaufort.

Had he settled for a slightly inebriated mediocrity, Jean-Luc might have stayed put for the rest of his working life. Instead, having wooed a waitress just out of college then lost her to one of his commis, he damped down his seething anger with just enough booze to undermine his competence. His temper grew shorter. The owners turned a blind eye to his cuffing the younger staff. When the hotel lost its star, however, they advised their chef that he would have to seek a position elsewhere though of course they would furnish him with first class references.

Accelerating decline followed. Early on, each fall from grace left Jean-Luc with a brief sense of elation that he had escaped from a trap. Later, as the job descriptions minced themselves into a pâté of drunken memories, whenever he was fired he merely felt relief that he need not show up for work the next day.

During a short stay in prison in Aix-en-Provence, sentenced for an assault he could not remember committing, he sobered up sufficiently to realize that whatever else happened with the rest of his life he was never going back to work in a professional kitchen. On his release he moved in with another ex-inmate who had inherited his family home, a small terraced house in Cavaillon.

At first they lived by selling the surplus furniture either to antique and second-hand dealers or by advertising in the local paper. When they were reduced to a kitchen table, two chairs and a bed, they reckoned, over a breakfast glass of red wine, that either the house would have to be sold or they would have to make money.

Pascal opted for thieving. Jean-Luc, who knew they would end up back inside if they went down that route, dissuaded him. They would start a business making preserves, hawk them to hotels, and do the markets at Apt, Gordes and L'Isle-sur-la-Sorgue. They could buy fruit for next to nothing. This was the fruit capital of France. All they needed was wheels.

Pascal caught a morning train to Marseille. That evening he parked a battered 2CV Camionette outside the front door. Jean-Luc asked no questions, not even when his partner switched number plates.

Having bought cheap job-lots of fruit at the end of trading from Cavaillon's wholesale market, they set to work making jam. Relying on a single propane burner and a maslin pan, they boiled up small batches of the ripe apricots, white peaches, oranges and melons that happened to be available. They took their entire stock to the nearest market, Coustallet, sold out by midday and had blown most of their takings on a champagne lunch by mid-afternoon. Celebrations apart, it was a routine they managed to sustain throughout the summer into autumn. They never found the energy to go out and sell their wares to the chic Provençal hostelries that pepper the Vaucluse, but one or two approached them with orders that they filled.

Once the tourists had gone, their initiative sputtered. It would have gone out too, except that a fellow-market-trader persuaded the two men to buy some overripe bananas, then some chestnuts, then some dates, then some pineapples from the Ivory Coast. Jean-Luc, having raked through the dregs of his experience as a chef, transformed them into a vanilla, cocoa and banana preserve, a chestnut and honey spread and a date, orange blossom and cinnamon chutney. The pineapple and Pinacolada recipe he devised bombed, but his other experiments did well enough in the larger towns to justify weekly visits.

It started as a game. Over breakfast of coffee and *vin du Luberon*, Pascal challenged Jean-Luc to invent preserves that not even the dumbest Japanese tourist would be prepared to buy.

'Seaweed and watermelon,' he came back. 'Nothing, nothing won't work so long as you tart it up in the right way.'

Pascal took the marker pen they used to label their pots and printed the words on the kitchen wall.

'Toothpaste and red currant jelly, ' Jean-Luc continued. 'Juniper and wild boar jam…apple and tangerine marmalade…sorrel and arbutus paste…kiwi with ginseng…rosemary and red mullet pickle… tamarind syrup.'

'Hold it. Hold it there!' Pascal ran the marker pen over the greying whitewash.

'Don't you understand,' Jean-Luc interrupted. 'There's nothing to it. It's child's play. Anybody could do it.'

'I couldn't,' Pascal said.

'You can't boil an egg.'

Their wall filled with culinary graffiti, designed with its own logic. Treble-circles drawn around an idea reflected inspiration. Double underlining marked ones that would almost certainly work. A practical recipe merited a single underscore. Words were scratched out, never to be revived. Drunken concepts were decorated with five-pointed stars or smiley faces.

As soon as the migrating vacationers returned, Jean-Luc translated his off-the-wall fancies into reality – at least some of them: orange and rosemary marmalade à la franglaise, rhubarb and wild strawberry semi-conserve, almond milk jam. They charged according to how they felt, their tariffs set according to whether they fancied a customer or took an irrational dislike to someone. If they wanted to go to a restaurant, they upped their prices to cover the meal.

What never changed was their way of working, still with the maslin pan and the single burner. Often the contents of their jars were still hot when they loaded them into their van, filled with mirabelles they had bought at four the same morning or a nectarine compote which they had boiled with a couple of bottles of red wine from Oppède, better than it needed to be, but chosen because they liked drinking it themselves.

Imperceptibly, their life-style altered. The market over, instead of gravitating to familiar bars around Cavaillon station where alcoholics tippled companionably, they would take a demijohn into the maquis with bread, saucisson and hard *picodon* cheese. Never quite sober yet perfectly content, they would stumble around the rocky hillsides, gathering savory, hyssop, fennel and juniper to carry back to their kitchen laboratory.

Pascal was manning their stall alone when the American woman stopped to make some purchases. She was, she volunteered, staying at a hotel in Gordes. After she had given him the name, he had no compunction in asking twice what he had intended charging her. Unfazed, she took away a pot of every variety they had brought that day. This wasn't unusual. Nor was it unexpected that she should ask him in which of the other markets they traded.

What was surprising was to meet her the next morning at Fontaine-de-Vaucluse, early when some of the late-arriving stallholders were still setting up. She wasn't alone. A man, obviously a photographer from the weight of bags he had slung around his neck kept pace with her, stopping to unpack cameras or change lenses and taking shots according to her directions.

'A journalist?' Pascal asked Jean-Luc.

'Sure.'

'She going to interview us, take our pictures, put us in a magazine?'

'Find out soon enough, she's coming here.'

The woman held out her hand to Pascal. Jean-Luc sized her up, sleek, successful, wearing her middle age comfortably. She was confident too, bright, not bothering to disguise her pleasure at having found a story.

'And you are the genius who creates these stunning, stunning preserves?' She unzipped a smile while searching for eye-contact with Jean-Luc.

'Who do you write for?' he asked.

She named a famous New York monthly: 'I'm its editor.'

He remembered the name. It had photographed his food for an Indonesian travel feature.

From nowhere, he felt an intense pang of nausea in his guts, like smelling a decomposing cat when emerging from a hangover.

'I'd like to write a feature about you, biography, where you buy your produce, your recipes of course, get some shots of your workshop; maybe we could go into the hills and photograph you picking herbs. Lavender would be great.'

Jean-Luc didn't try and keep up. He didn't do enthusiasm any more.

He held up his hand. 'Hold on madam. Look, I don't want to be impolite. Let's just say that we aren't interested in press coverage. If you want to take our picture now, we don't mind, but that's it.'

'You don't want publicity?'

'Why should we? Do we want publicity?' Jean-Luc turned to Pascal.

'Wouldn't do us much good,' he shrugged.

'We're just amateurs, part-timers. To put it bluntly we haven't registered ourselves as a business. We don't pay taxes. Nobody bothers us. That suits us fine.'

'But you are unique,' the woman interrupted. 'You are doing things with jams and jellies that nobody else would dream of. They're not just clever. Give me credit for recognizing something that's out on its own.'

Jean-Luc noticed that the photographer was snapping him while he talked. He looked more closely at his interviewer: determined, powerful, persistent. For the first time in a long while, he took an executive decision.

'Piss off!' he said.

And she did.

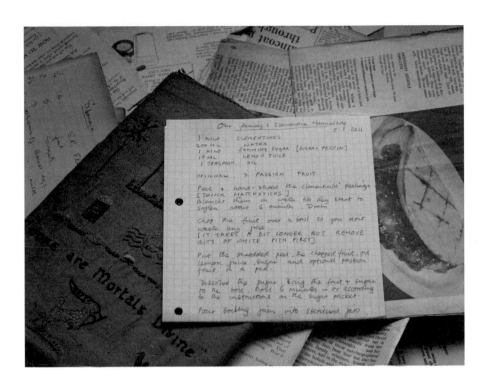

not so wild strawberries

The most quotable quote on the subject of strawberries is Dr William Butler's, 'God could have made a better berry, but doubtless never did,' which is probably why the only way of picking them for any length of time is on one's knees, something I know about, having spent a summer in the Cotswolds as a piece-worker on a farm with twenty-five acres of Cambridge Favourites. At the end of the day, having filled my self-imposed quota of sixteen sixteen-pound trays, I'd fall asleep and dream bright red strawberry-coloured dreams.

Those immaculate fields were weed- and pest-free, quite unlike the unkempt beds, patches and clusters we now grow. Our tiny alpines self-seed on the paths between rows of beans, onions and artichokes. Bindweed tangles with the runners of our larger berries. Up close, while we pick, we expose brown and yellow snails, resting satiated on the leaves. They have a knack for feeding off the sweetest fruit, leaving behind traces of their diligent quarrying. Their taste is faultless. Eat a strawberry attacked by any form of wild-life; it will be sweeter than the untouched one beside it.

Alpines are fragile. They bruise easily. It takes delicate fingers to pluck them from their stems. They're often called wild strawberries even though cultivated. Some are pimple-small, others the size of a thumbnail. Some are dry, almost bitter, others tart and juicy, others perfumed like attar of roses. Their taste is evanescent. Leave a packed container in the fridge for a couple of days and the aroma will have dulled perceptibly. The best way of enjoying them is to treat them like sweeties while working in the garden on a hot summer's day: dig a bit, weed a bit then plug one's mouth with a handful.

Large, luscious strawberries, the kind that are swamped with cream, are blowsy by comparison, less élitist. What most cooks can throw at them, they can take. Forty-year-old *aceto balsamico tradizionale*: why not? A bottle of Brouilly: *pourquoi pas*? Dipped in chocolate couverture, sprinkled with black pepper, baked in a crumble with rhubarb, crushed in an Eton mess, or packed into a summer pudding, they retain some vestige of their essence. Victims of their own popularity, they have to put up with the indignities accompanying it.

Only one form of abuse seems inexcusable. Check into a luxury hotel and the chances are that, whatever the season, a basket of fresh fruit is waiting for guests in their rooms and that, placed neatly between orange, apple and banana, will be a seductive scarlet strawberry. More cabbage than fruit, more cardboard than juice, devoid of fragrance, it's an edible lie. Room service would do better to replace it with a wax facsimile; at least it would be re-usable.

In Regency times, large houses occasionally decorated their dining tables with pots of wild-strawberry-bearing plants for diners to help themselves. As a gesture, it has a natural elegance to it. Jane Austen would doubtless have approved.

STRAWBERRIES IN VANILLA SYRUP

125g caster sugar • 140ml approx water • 1 vanilla pod
500g strawberries • ½ lemon

Heat sugar, water and vanilla in a small pan. Simmer 10 minutes
without boiling. Chill to just above freezing. Roughly chop the
strawberries. Squeeze a little lemon juice over them. Pour over the
syrup. Chill no more than 30 minutes before serving.

STRAWBERRY AND RHUBARB SOUP

200g sugar • 3 strips of lemon rind • 300g rhubarb
300g strawberries • 100g Alpine strawberries

Put the sugar in a pan with lemon rind and 250ml water. Add roughly
chopped rhubarb. Poach until tender, Cool. Remove lemon rind.
Liquidize with strawberries and chill. Serve as a soup garnished with
Alpine strawberries.

STRAWBERRY AND RASPBERRY SORBET

450g raspberries • 450g mixed alpine and other strawberries
300g caster sugar

Put the raspberries in a sieve. Force the pulp through it, but not the
seeds. Add splashes of water to extract most of the pulp. Liquidize
raspberries, strawberries and sugar. Leave until the sugar has dissolved.
Churn in an ice-cream maker.

ALPINE STRAWBERRY CRÉMETS

1 egg white • 50g caster sugar • 250ml double cream
100g *fromage blanc* • 100g strawberries • 100g alpine strawberries

Whisk egg white and 25g sugar until stiff. Whisk cream until stiff. Line four *coeur à la crème* moulds with muslin. Fold cream, *fromage blanc* and egg white together. Spoon into the muslin. Stand on a plate. Refrigerate at least 3 hours and turn out. Liquidize strawberries, half the alpines and the remaining sugar. Spoon the sauce around the crémets. Sprinkle the rest of the alpines on it.

wild plums

'Wild plums from the Drift, A. up tree, plum-almond tartlets....also omelette with blue eggs from P.L, field mushrooms and ceps.'

[Tweet-speak]

It's like looking down the wrong end of a telescope. Details diminish to an out-of-focus memory. Bits are recoverable: three trees growing in a hedge beside a rugby pitch; the plums small, round, blush-red; clambering into a ditch and pulling at the lower branches to pick them; hooking an umbrella handle round a branch just out of reach; filling a rucksack; noticing that blackberries clustered around a trunk were starting to ripen.

And the tartlets? By force of habit, remembering them is easier: a reduced plum compote coating a crisp *pâte brisée*, a layer of almond frangipane and a bright red glaze made from the sweetened juice. It looked garish to the point of being ugly but it tasted so good.

Although the rest may have faded to a blur, it triggers vivid flash-backs, yellow plums that spilled onto the pavement beside a main road, a purple *quetsche* that stained the ground around it with splashes of purple over-ripe fruit, and golden *mirabelles* on an abandoned property in the Loiret that were sweet as honey.

Sloes are plums too, albeit no bigger than cherries. Yes, they make a kind of gin, more of a liqueur because they aren't fermented, merely macerated in alcohol. But they're more than a one-recipe wonder. They also make interesting fruit vinegar. The astringency that characterizes them in their raw state dissipates once they've been steeped for a few weeks. Boiling gets rid of it too. They turn out a powerful, dark jelly, every bit as interesting as red currant, when dished up with venison or lamb.

It isn't just the wild ones that stick in the mind. My Polish mother-in-law once produced an unforgettable chilled greengage soup – stewed and sieved *Reine Claudes*, sugar, raw milk, nothing else. A step-great aunt who lived in an echoing rectory had a cook, Hilda, who baked juicy Victorias under an old-fashioned piecrust made with lard: delicious hot, better served cold with thick cream. Damson jam, denser than most other preserves and slightly acid, is unique. In a dark recess of our larder a few jars of menacing, dark brown plum chutney spiked with cinnamon, cloves and allspice (vintage 1980-something) are still waiting to be broached.

Dusting down these souvenirs isn't altogether arbitrary. Figuratively speaking a 'Plum' signifies something desirable and special, but that isn't how people think about plums routinely. They've slipped into a neglected middle ground, neither taken for granted like apples, say, or bananas nor granted a special status like strawberries and raspberries. Probably, they're more popular eaten as prunes. Because they are disregarded, they have the power of surprise when they turn out to be far better than expected.

One final mental picture emerges. It's picking or cutting the stones out of the wild plums. Whether they're ripe or still a little green, whether left raw or cooked first, it's a fiddly, messy job.

YELLOW WILD PLUM PIE

PASTRY

250g flour • 140g salted butter
1 egg • 60g sugar

Crumb flour and butter together. Mix eggs and sugar. Work into the flour and butter to form a ball. Rest.

PIE

butter for greasing • 700g yellow plums • 140g sugar
15g cornflour • 400g pastry • 1tbs semolina • egg yolk

Grease a 25cm tart ring with butter. Preheat oven to 190°C. Wash the plums and stir-fry them slowly in a wok until they split. Remove the stones. Add sugar. Dust with cornflour. Roll out three-quarters of the pastry and line the tart ring. Sprinkle semolina over it. Spread the fruit over the base. Roll out the rest of the pastry to make a lid. Seal by crimping the moistened edges. Brush the top with yolk. Bake 40 minutes. Eat warm.

PLUM AND ALMOND TARTLETS

PÂTE BRISÉE

80g chilled butter • 160g plain flour • 2–3tbs iced water

Cut the butter into small cubes. Mix it with the flour, but don't crumb it. Add the water and work into a dough leaving streaks of butter in it.

FRANGIPANE

60g butter • 60g caster sugar • 60g beaten egg
2 drops almond essence • 70g ground almonds

Cream the butter and 60g sugar. Incorporate egg, essence and almonds.

TARTS

350g wild plums • 120 g sugar • butter for greasing
pâte brisée • 4tsp semolina • frangipane

Stew the plums with sugar and half a cup of water. Strain them in a sieve over a clean pan. Stone them. Boil the liquid to a glaze. Grease four 10cm tartlet tins. Line with rolled-out pastry. Preheat oven to 200°C. Sprinkle semolina on the pastry bases. Spread plums on top. Cover with frangipane and bake about 30 minutes. Brush with hot glaze and cool.

SLOE AND JAPONICA JELLY

900g japonica • zest of 1 lemon • 450g sloes
850g pectin sugar per litre of juice

Slice the japonica thinly – like cucumber. Put it in a large pan with lemon and 1400ml water. Boil until it softens and then add the sloes. Continue boiling until their skins split. Strain the juice through a jelly bag overnight. Put the juice in a clean pan with pectin sugar. Stir to dissolve and boil hard for 6 minutes. Pour into sterilized jars and seal.

easy as apple pie

Making apple pie wasn't always easy. One fourteenth-century recipe, for instance, would challenge plenty of cooks today. Part of the apple was blended with wine. The rest was chopped up and combined with onions, figs, raisins and spices (possibly pine kernels too). An addition of fried onions might seem weird to us, but caramelized they're sweet. Baked in a double-crusted pie, glazed with saffron, the mixture would have tasted something like exotic *apfel strudel*.

In contrast, a branded modern pie-let, fresh from its convenience packaging, offers glue-textured, sweetened Bramley in neutered pastry, dusted with sugar. Only a factory could clone such a product by the million and get away with it.

Somewhere between ancient and modern, between Taillevent's court cuisine and mass appeal, the treasure of a half-decent apple pie lies buried. Its secret is adaptability, jazz-able to the nth degree, as exclusive or commonplace as cooks want it to be, so long as they adhere to the basic precept: use apples that taste good.

This injunction alone could fill a book. Culinary or cooking apples are acid. They collapse into a mush when boiled. Some table apples, Cox's for instance, which are related to the French Reine des Reinettes, may look great sliced up as a *tarte aux pommes* but will fill a pie with chunks and lumps. Between these extremes there are hundreds, literally, of varieties that work. Within walking distance of our house I can forage for about a dozen, most of which would challenge an experienced pomologist.

Along the old railway line that's been turned into a cycle path is one tree that sprays a carpet of cider apples on the ground. They're hard and inedible, designed for juicing. Another tree produces orange and red-flecked fruit that tastes, if anything, worse, even though cows seem to like it. A third supplies a crop of green bullets, too hard to munch but ideal when cooked. A fourth, also, I suspect, primarily a cider apple, is crisp and juicy with a hint of sweetness. And there are three more trees in the nearby hamlet of Chaffcombe, one in the churchyard and two in the pound, one of which has yellow apples hanging on its branches until December.

All this is leading up to my case that it's better to stew the apples before loading them in the pastry. This way you can sweeten them *quanto basto*, drain any excess moisture from them and combine chunky pieces with sloshy, crumbled bits. And you play with this base as the spirit moves you. Grated japonica, a relative of quince, adds a special fragrance, but so do lemon zests. Cinnamon creates one effect, cloves another. Raw blackcurrants or blackberries mixed with the cooked apple will keep their texture in the pie.

Pre-cooking tacks on an extra benefit. On a double-crusted pie the base has to be baked. If it's not, it turns into something akin to a wet nappy. How a paste bakes depends in part on its container and in part on the oven. The thing to avoid though is juice leeching into it. If the texture of the filling has been sorted, the chances of half-decent pastry improve.

APPLE PIE WITH STRUDEL FILLING

SHORTCRUST PASTRY

250g flour • pinch of salt • 70g soft butter
60g lard • 30ml (approx.) milk

Sift flour and salt. Crumb with fats. Add water and form into a dough.

THE PIE

500g culinary apples • 150g sugar and 1 extra tbs to glaze
2 cloves • ground cinnamon to taste
60g sultanas • 20g butter • shortcrust paste
2tbs semolina. • 1tbs milk to glaze

Peel, core and chop the apples. Stew them with sugar, cloves and 100ml water. When they've collapsed, add cinnamon and sultanas. Cool. Preheat oven to 200°C. Butter a 25cm tart ring. Line with two-thirds of the pastry. Sprinkle semolina over it. Spread apple on top. Roll out the rest of the pastry for a lid. Fit on top and crimp the edges to seal. Brush with milk and sprinkle with sugar. Bake for 35 minutes.

APPLE AND RED CURRANT CRUMBLE

200g self-raising flour • 100g butter • 50g soft brown sugar
700g well-flavoured apples • 250g frozen red currants
180g sugar

Crumb the flour and butter. When it gets sandy add a splash of water. Go on mixing so there are a few lumps. Mix in the sugar. Preheat the oven to 190°C. Peel, core and roughly chop the apples. Spread them over the base of an ovenproof dish. Sprinkle the crumble over the top – not too thick. Bake for 50 minutes.

APPLE AND JAPONICA PIES

SHORTCRUST PASTRY

150g flour • pinch of salt • 50g soft butter
25g lard • 20ml (approx.) water

Sift flour and salt. Crumb with fats. Add water and form into a dough.

THE PIES

500g well-flavoured apples • 150g sugar • 1 grated japonica
250g shortcrust pastry • 4tsp semolina
2tbs milk • butter for greasing

Peel, core and quarter apples. Stew with very little water and 125g sugar until soft. Stir in the japonica and cool. Grease four 10cm tartlet rings. Preheat oven to 200°C. Roll out pastry and line the rings. Trim edges. Roll out trimmings and left-over dough for pie lids. Sprinkle semolina over bases. Spoon apple into tartlets. Moisten edges, fit lids and crimp. Brush with milk. Dust with sugar. Bake for 20–25 minutes.

Quince instead of japonica achieves an almost identical result.

roll it thin

In a kitchen drawer there are two sets of battens, one 2mm and the other 3mm thick. They date back to a time when I practised pastry making with uncharacteristic care. The trick was to put a batten on either side of a slab of dough and roll it out until the pin was touching the two strips of wood. That way the pastry was always uniform and at the desired thickness.

Why the precision? More often than not we throw together more pastry than we need and also more often than not we're tempted into rolling it out too thick. This has to be linked to some deep-rooted folk memory, in which pride in baking plays a part, but it's allied to recipe compilers' beliefs that they have to add a margin of tolerance so the more ham-fisted among us will still manage some kind of result.

Without being strudel skinny, two millimetres doesn't seem much, but it's what pâtissiers use for smaller tarts and tartlets while three millimetres does for larger ones. They take it for granted that pastry is a shell designed to hold a filling. Go back three centuries, and treatises on the art of cookery seem to dismiss these containers by referring to them as 'coffins'.

Rolling thin doesn't undervalue pastry. It still has to be short, crisp, brittle or puffed as opposed to tough, soggy, raw or deflated. It has to be fresh and taste good. Battens or no, it isn't possible to do a half-way competent job on it without some basic craftsmanship. All sorts of 'rules' spring to mind: 'Don't force the pastry out'; 'Don't roll over the edges'; 'Roll in the same direction'; 'Turn the dough after each roll, ... 45° for circles and 90° for rectangles'; 'Don't over flour the work-surface'; 'Work with cool hands'; 'Always rest pastry before baking'.

Some, if not all, of these dos and don'ts can be broken without botching the job. Each of them has merit. Even a maladroit cook like me sticks to them except when in a tearing hurry and the outcome, then, is never as good.

Along the line too, wheezes slip into the memory-bank. Sugar-crust pastry, always at risk of breaking because of its high fat-content, pins out more easily between two sheets of film. Dock the raw dough before lining a tart ring and line it with the pricked surface downwards – it bakes better and doesn't blister. Leaving any flaps of spare dough hanging over the sides of the tin protects, up to a point, against shrinkage.

This isn't meant to come across as a covert lesson in the art of pâtisserie. There are umpteen instances where 'thick' is beautiful: pasties, for instance, or raised pies. It is a plea in support of home bakers who think beyond the branded products in freezer cabinets, however reliable these may be. Rubbing fat and flour between thumb and forefinger is a soothing meditation, better than the yoga class at a health centre.

SMOKED SALMON AND CREAM CHEESE TARTLETS

RICH SHORTCRUST PASTRY

270g flour • 160g salted butter • 70g beaten egg

This paste is made in a food processor. Crumb the flour and butter. Add the egg. Process until the dough comes away from the sides of the bowl.

THE TARTS

butter for greasing • 320g rich shortcrust pastry
1tsp Dijon mustard • squeeze of lemon juice • 1 egg and 1 yolk
150ml double cream • 4 slices smoked salmon
80g cream cheese

Butter four 10cm tartlet tins. Line tins with pastry. Cover with greaseproof. Fill with baking beans. Bake blind for 20 minutes at 180°C. Cool. Raise oven temperature to 230°C. Beat together mustard, lemon, egg and cream. Put salmon in each pastry shell. Dab cream cheese on top. Pour over the cream and bake about 20 minutes.

LEEK TART

PÂTE BRISÉE

100g chilled butter • 180g flour • 4tbs iced water

Cut the butter into small cubes. Mix it with the flour, but don't crumb it. Add the water and work into a dough leaving streaks of butter in it.

THE TART

700g diced leeks • 60g butter • salt
2 eggs and 2 yolks • 300ml whipping cream

Line a greased 26cm tart tin with pastry. Cover with greaseproof. Fill with baking beans. Bake blind for 20 minutes at 180°C. Sweat the leeks in butter with salt until they're soft. Spread over the pastry base. Whisk eggs, yolks and cream and pour over leeks. Bake 30–40 minutes until just set.

RHUBARB TART

500g maincrop rhubarb • 120g sugar • 1 large sliver orange zest
1 star anis • 240g flour • 10g cornflour • 130g butter
50g icing sugar • 1 egg

Chop the rhubarb into 3cm pieces. Boil 300ml water and sugar with orange and star anis about 3 minutes. Add rhubarb and simmer until it starts to mush. Empty the rhubarb into a sieve over a clean pan. Reduce syrup to a glaze. Mix half with rhubarb in a bowl. Sift flour, cornflour and icing sugar. Rub in butter. Add beaten egg and make a pastry dough. Line a 20cm tart ring with two-thirds of it. Rest 20 minutes. Preheat oven to 180°C. Spread rhubarb over pastry base. Cover with a lattice made from remaining pastry. Bake for 50 minutes. Brush top with any left-over rhubarb glaze.

You'll have about 150g raw pastry left over.

runny custard

'*Vanilla sauce from milk or cream for pudding or cauliflower* – 2 *glasses cream, milk or sour cream, 3–4 pieces sugar, 4–5 egg yolks, ½ vershok vanilla or cinnamon.*'

Elena Molokhovets, *A Gift To Young Housewives*, 1861, translated as *Classic Russian Cooking* by Joyce Toomre (Indiana University Press, 1992).

Encouraging a newly-wed to pour custard on cauliflower is the kind of gift that belongs in a catalogue of mother-in-law jokes. The recipe itself, though, isn't unlike the one you'd find in a Mrs Beeton, past or present, or Escoffier – though he called it *crème anglaise* – or even a modern culinary swami's.

Without its ½ *vershok* of vanilla (1 *vershok* is 4.45 cm), custard forms a background, a colour, a texture, a level of sweetness and a diluted egg yolk taste. Like the wash a watercolour artist brushes across his paper, it's a base.

It's what happens to custard next that makes it interesting. The limitless palette of ice-cream (churned, frozen custard) shows it doesn't take a Turner to invent a new taste. Stem ginger, prunes in armagnac, Kurdish pistachio nuts, tonka beans, single-estate Venezuelan Criolla chocolate, marmalade, bacon and egg – only imagination dictates where to draw the line.

Scientists have evolved two mind-addling formulas for the perfect soft-boiled egg. They had the same aim: to set the white, the albumen, without the yolk hardening. One reached his conclusions by measuring mass, the other an egg's circumference. They agreed that critical changes to its structure take place between 62°C and 69°C, but reached different conclusions about the time.

Their experience translates to the tricks of custard-making. Overheat it while it's simmering on the stove and the yolks will curdle, but working with an electronic probe to measure temperature can be misleading too. Being an alert cook beats half-baked science. Technique outpoints technology.

The pan: a thick-bottomed saucepan that heats evenly will warm the mixture more evenly. Aluminium turns custard grey.

The spoon or spatula: stirring throughout is critical. Some kind of straight-edged tool that lets you work around the edges where the base joins the sides deals with hotspots.

Whisking: whisking sugar and eggs until they whiten before adding hot milk or cream gives an extra margin of tolerance.

'When is the custard ready?' is the key question. There is no single specific response. The old manuals used to say, 'When it coats the back of a wooden spoon', in other words, as soon as it thickens. This was usually allied to a severe warning not to let it boil. The latter advice holds good, but doesn't give the full picture. At 69°C – remember the scientists with their egg-boiling experiments – the sauce begins to cook. It continues to gain 'body' without curdling to 80-odd degrees. By then, though still fluid, it has a marked consistency and, when cooled, it thickens.

Without flavouring, thicker or runnier, it's still a neutral 'wash'. Without the cook's personal touch it lacks character. The '½ *vershok* vanilla', for instance, can transform it in more ways than one. Infusing it in hot milk or cream for a few minutes will do one thing; infusing it and leaving it to stand overnight, another. Splitting it first will change the way it delivers its unique hit. Scraping out the seeds will change the custard's appearance. Tahitian vanilla doesn't have the same taste as Madagascan. Some cooks happily add one or even two whole pods to a pint of milk. Like curry that improves if it's set aside, custard ripens over a day or so.

RUNNY CUSTARD

500ml unskimmed milk • 1 split vanilla pod
60–80g caster sugar (according to taste) • 4 or 5 egg yolks

Bring the milk and vanilla to the boil. Leave to stand for 5 minutes. Whisk the yolks and sugar in a bowl until they whiten. Whisk the milk onto the eggs. Rinse the pan and dry it. Pour the custard back into it. Over a low heat, stirring with a wooden spoon, heat the custard until it thickens slightly. To tell when it's ready, the sauce should coat the back of the spoon and, if you draw your finger through it, there's a clear divide. (The critical thickening temperature is between 82°C and 85°C.) Take the sauce off the heat and stand it on a cold surface, so the pan base cools.

Any pan but aluminium is good.

STEM GINGER ICE-CREAM

120g stem ginger in syrup • 200ml double cream
400ml chilled custard

Blend the chopped ginger, syrup and cream in a food processor. Combine with the custard. Churn and freeze in an ice-cream machine.

SILKY CHOCOLATE CUSTARD

120ml milk • 120ml double cream • 1 split vanilla pod
1 egg • 1tsp cornflour • 30g caster sugar
60g grated dark chocolate

Simmer the milk, cream and vanilla 10 minutes. Remove the vanilla pod. Beat the egg, cornflour and sugar in a bowl until smooth. Whisk the milk and cream onto them. Return to the pan and stir until the custard boils. Add the chocolate and let it melt. Use a stick-blender to blitz it while hot. The custard becomes shiny. Pour into custard cups or ramekins and chill.

BAKED EGG CUSTARD

2tbs milk • softened unsalted butter • 400ml whipping cream
4 egg yolks • 60g caster sugar • 1tsp vanilla essence
1 nutmeg

Brush a saucepan with milk. Butter a small (1–1½ pint) pie dish. Preheat the oven to 150°C. Bring the cream to the boil in the pan. Whisk yolks, sugar and vanilla in a bowl until creamy. Beat in the cream and strain into the pie dish. Bake for 50 minutes or until set. Grate a whole nutmeg over the custard's surface.

PASSION FRUIT CUSTARDS

80g caster sugar • 170ml passion fruit juice
2 eggs and 2 yolks • 120ml very fresh double cream

Preheat the oven to 150°C. Whisk sugar with the fruit juice until it dissolves. Beat thoroughly with the eggs. Add the double cream. (If it isn't fresh it will curdle!) Pour into four 125ml ramekins. Stand them in a pan with hot water half way up their sides. Bake until set, about 40 minutes. Cool before serving.

cream

It used to be a luxury. Now it costs less than cheap olive oil. The cream of 'cream cakes', 'strawberries and cream' and 'cream sauces' used to flag up epicurean indulgence. Not any more. At a pinch 'cream teas' slip through fashion's net as a retro-treat. Ice-cream is ever-popular, but hardly luxurious. Disguised with a designer label as *crème fraîche*, it can waddle up the culinary catwalk. This decline in status coincides with a phase when *mascarpone*, a word that's smooth as treacle and pumped full of saturated fat, struts its stuff unchallenged.

Cream tastes of very little, so it's fair to challenge its worth. What has it going for it? Two answers. One is mouth-feel. Hot or cold, it paints the palate. It's uniquely tactile. It lingers in the mouth. The other, and it's closely related, is its ability to carry other flavours, to absorb vivid colours and soften them into pastel shades. In a *gratin dauphinois* the smidgeon of garlic percolates through the cream and potato to turn something inherently bland into something moreish.

Margaret Costa, a *grand dame* of Britain's cookery writing sorority, wrote an enlightened chapter on cooking with cream for her *Four Seasons Cookery Book*. In it she used cream a lot – as opposed to a lot of cream – because she liked simple food. 'Too much,' she said, 'is a sign of vulgarity in restaurant cooking and ignorance in a home.'

Written at a time when the country was still emerging from the austerity years that followed World War II, it prefigured two decades of abusive cream-soaked cuisine that explains why so few talented chefs use it for anything other than the odd crème brûlée, parfait or custard tart today. Those dishes have lasted the course, become classics because they're good, but also for a less obvious reason.

Eggs have a natural affinity with cream. Recipes combining the two run to thousands. They work in tandem, blanketing an extended family of dishes that range from *quiches* to *bavarois*, from *sabayons* to *mousselines* and from *gâteaux de riz* to *profiteroles*. If that seems like a list extrapolated from a Cordon Bleu manifesto, so be it. They reflect a style of cookery that stresses richness, no bad thing, so long as it doesn't degenerate into an artery-blocking norm.

Cream wasn't designed to be a routine ingredient, the open pot on the middle shelf of the fridge, waiting to be spooned onto every pudding or poured into every thick soup. It's case-specific. Just because half a pint of double cream makes a banana ice-cream to die for, twice as much will not make it any better. There will be recipes to splash out – the sticky part of a sticky toffee pudding; recipes to go easy – scrambled eggs, where a spoonful added off the heat drops the temperature and prevents them overcooking; food where it's essential – clotted cream with scones and strawberry jam; food where it's redundant – fruit salad. As Margaret Costa implied, it deserves to be respected, treated with a degree of subtlety.

ANT'S GOAT'S CHEESE MOUSSE

220g dried brown breadcrumbs • 2tsp finely chopped rosemary
salt • 60g melted butter • 1 sachet gelatine
300g fresh goat's cheese • 300ml double cream
100g ground almonds • 60g basil purée or pesto

Mix breadcrumbs, rosemary and a little salt with butter. Line a flan
ring with the mixture as per a cheesecake. Dissolve gelatine in a little
hot water. Combine with the goat's cheese. Whisk the double cream
until firm. Fold into the goat's cheese. Spread over the crumbs. Leave
to set. Combine ground almonds and basil. Spread over the mousse
before serving.

VANILLA PARFAIT

6 egg yolks • 100g vanilla sugar • 600ml double cream

Whisk the yolks until they froth. Add the sugar and continue whisking
until the mixture thickens. In another bowl whisk the cream until it
holds its shape. Fold into the egg and sugar. Churn in an ice-cream
machine.

AND THEN VARY BY ADDING.....

...oven-dried wholemeal bread crumbs

...very ripe bananas

...marmalade

...armagnac

...hazelnut praline, etc.

CHOCOLATE AND BANANA CREAM

75g grated dark chocolate • 1 shot espresso or strong black coffee
150g ripe banana • 1tbs soft brown sugar
150g Greek yoghurt • 250ml double cream

Melt the chocolate in the microwave oven. Add the coffee, mashed banana and sugar. Cool and fold in the yoghurt. Whisk the double cream and fold into the mixture. Pour into glass dishes, chill and serve.

bacon knuckles

It's all about market forces. One day the butcher couldn't give them away and the next, the lamb shank, chicken wing, pig's trotter or skate cheeks costs more than a boned-out arm and leg put together. Ounce for ounce, the meat on oxtail costs more than fillet steak. Stitch on the trimmings needed to make it yummy and the hours of simmering before it falls of the bone and it's a luxury.

Actually, these odds and ends become fashionable in the long run for a reason. They're more interesting than a slab of grilled meat; they bring more interest, more pleasure. The person sitting at the dinner table who refuses the parson's nose on a roasted chicken doesn't understand taste or texture. The same applies to anyone binning a salmon head. When authority bans giblets it closes the door on a *salade de gésiers confits*, poultry stomach-muscles simmered until tender in duck fat, one of the great joys of French peasant cookery.

I hear that beef tripe goes to the cosmetics industry – guts into slap. In England, at any rate, it vanished from our kitchens when large, approved abattoirs forced the closure of local slaughterhouses. And it wasn't just the loss of that ugly slab of bleached tripe wallowing in a slough of gluey white sauce. Ruminants have four stomachs, each one with a different texture, one plain, one like towelling, another like a brown accordion and a fourth like honeycomb.

Bacon knuckles haven't yet seeped into the repertoire of once-ignored, now-in-the-spotlight bits of animal, but it's only a matter of time. The fore-hocks from which they're severed at the joint have already risen in the rankings. Glamour-puss chefs convert them into terrines, layering them with lobes of foie gras, an alternative to pigs' trotters, poached, boned and stuffed with sweetbreads and morels.

The only trouble with knuckles is that, smoked or green, they're too salty. They have to soak overnight before they're fit. Afterwards, they'll do for anything, from soups and stews to pâtés, so long as they're cooked slowly. What they have going for them is a lip-salve gelatinous texture, better than a hock's, with more flesh than a trotter.

Split pea soup can be dreary, leaving its furry film in the mouth, but it doesn't have to be. Simmered in a knuckle broth, pulses become suave and velvety. A couple of smoked knuckles make better brawn than any pig's head ... but with a proviso. The amount of rind on them forms a kind of surgical stocking, more than most of us would happily eat. Once the meat is tender, the outer layer of rind doesn't serve much purpose. Carving it off and binning it is one solution. However, if you abhor waste, put it in the bottom of a casserole when making a stew. The residual gelatine will improve the sauce without changing its flavour (some old recipes for daubes start off by instructing the cook to line the pot with pork rind).

HAM KNUCKLE TERRINE

2 ham or gammon knuckles • 1 large onion • 2 cloves
100g chopped celery • 150g chopped carrot • 1 bottle perry
300g cooked asparagus • salt

Soak the knuckles 24 hours in two changes of water. Stud onion with cloves. Put the knuckles, onion, celery and carrot in a saucepan. Cover with water and perry. Simmer about 2½ hours until the meat is almost falling off the bone. Strain a litre of liquid into a pan and reduce to 300ml. Adjust seasoning. Discard rind and bones. Cube the meat. Line a terrine with film. Spread half the meat over it. Cover with asparagus and the rest of the meat. Pour over the reduced stock. Weight the terrine, refrigerate overnight and turn out.

This may be served with a herb vinaigrette.

CANNELLINI BEANS AND BACON KNUCKLE

1 pre-soaked bacon knuckle • 500g cannellini beans, soaked overnight
500g sliced onions • 60ml olive oil • 60g tomato purée
400ml dry cider • 2 stock cubes • 2 bayleaves
4 sprigs rosemary • salt and pepper

Bathe the knuckle in cold water. Simmer until it comes off the bone easily – about 2½ hours. Take out of cooking liquid and pull away the rind. Fry onions in oil until transparent. Add to liquid. Drain the beans from their soaking water and boil them in fresh water for 10 minutes, then drain. Add them, the tomato purée, cider, stock cubes and herbs to the knuckle and broth. Simmer very gently until the beans soften. Top up with extra water as necessary. Add back the meat from the knuckle. Boil to reduce liquid. Season with salt (if needed) and plenty of pepper.

SPLIT PEA SOUP

1 pre-soaked smoked bacon knuckle • 60g oil • 250g diced onions
500g split peas, pre-soaked • 2 bayleaves • 1 small bunch of thyme
250g celeriac in small cubes • salt and pepper
20g chopped flat-leaf parsley

Bathe the knuckle in cold water. Simmer until it comes off the bone easily – about 2½ hours. Remove the rind and chop up the meat. Heat the oil in a large pan. Cook the onions until soft. Add the peas, bayleaves and thyme. Pour over the stock from the knuckle. Add water to make 3 litres. Put the bone in the soup and simmer 2 hours. Take out the bone, bayleaf and thyme. Add celeriac and chopped meat. Simmer 30 minutes more. Part blend the soup. Check seasoning. Finish with parsley.

bread and butter puddings

It's not as if there's only one kind of bread and butter pudding. There are hot ones, cold ones, spiced ones, fruity ones, ones with crunchy tops, ones spread with apricot jam, ones enriched with cream, ones baked with brioche or diet bread or sliced bread rolls and ones that swell like soufflés.

My favourite owes something to Mrs Beeton. Baked in a pie or a Pyrex dish, the top crisp and encrusted with demerara sugar, it's fluffy inside and pregnant with plumped sultanas. It's meant for eating fresh out of the oven. When it cools it sinks and solidifies, nice in its own way, but that's another story.

Bread and butter pudding intended for eating cold is richer, but more delicate, closer to a baked egg custard. It's what, ever since the Dorchester Grill served it half a century ago, celebrity chefs stick on their menus. Surprisingly, French pâtissiers have devised their own take, a single layer of buttered brioche triangles baked crisp in what's suspiciously like a *crème anglaise*.

For a hot pud., the choice of bread does affect the way it rises. Light, sliced loaves, the kind sold to weight-watchers, puff up like balloons. Leaving on the crusts makes the top crisper. Crispness isn't an issue for the 'cold' school. Providing it will soak up the liquid any bread will pass. Quite a few of these versions dispense with ovens and poach the pudding by standing it in a bain marie.

An old 'Granny says' rule about the milk and eggs was to beat them hard, pour them over the buttered bread and leave them to stand before cooking. Reading between the lines, it seems that the canny lady thought she was trapping as much air as she could.

The eggs–cream–milk method has an alternative agenda. Air and steam are anathema. Its aim is to set the protein. Boiling the mixture would ruin its texture. Butter spread evenly on the bread will, if it's a good one, improve the taste, but it's enriching a pudding that is already rich.

Eliza Smith, an early eighteenth-century Martha Stewart, was tailoring her advice to large households. Her 'Bread and Butter Pudding for Fasting-Days' raises an ironic smile:

> Take a two penny loaf, and a pound of fresh butter; spread it in very thin slices, as to eat; cut them off as you spread them, and stone half a pound of raisins, and wash a pound of currants; then put puff-paste at the bottom of a dish, and lay a row of your bread and butter, and strew a handful of currants, a few raisins, and some little bits of butter, and so do till your dish is full; then boil three pints of cream and thicken it when cold with the yolks of ten eggs, a grated nutmeg, a little salt, near half a pound of sugar, and some orange flower-water; pour this in just as the pudding is going into the oven.
>
> *The Compleat Housewife: or Accomplish'd Gentlewoman's Companion* (1st edition 1729, facsimile reprint 1968)

Apart from its scale, more likely to appeal to dinner ladies, it's appetizing from every point of view. Even the detail of the pastry case would work if the pudding was baked on the sole of a pizza oven.

In the early days of prime-time cookery programmes, the Swiss chef Anton Mossiman who dished up his interpretation received 60,000 requests for the recipe from viewers. It's hard to imagine another other old-fashioned standby generating that level of enthusiasm.

MRS B'S HOT BREAD AND BUTTER PUDDING

100–120g softened butter • 2 eggs • 500ml unskimmed milk
50g sugar • 10–12 slices diet bread • 200g sultanas
demerara sugar

Butter the sides of a two-pint pie dish. Preheat the oven to 200°C. Whisk the eggs, milk and sugar together for 5 minutes. Butter the bread, minus the crusts at both ends. Cut each slice into triangles. Soak them in the custard. Take them out as you go and line the dish. Sprinkle triangles with sultanas between layers. Leave to stand for an hour (Mrs B. is quite clear about the importance of this). Sprinkle demerara on top and bake 45–50 minutes.

BRIOCHE AND BUTTER PUDDING

1 small brioche loaf, about 250g • 60g softened unsalted butter
250ml milk • 250ml single cream • 4 eggs
100g caster sugar • 1tsp vanilla essence

Cut the brioche into thin slices and butter them. Toast them, buttered side only, until lightly coloured. Bring the milk and cream to the boil. Beat the eggs, sugar, and vanilla until creamy. Whisk in the hot milk. Pour half the custard into an ovenproof dish (which should be big enough to fit the brioche in a single overlapping layer). Cut the lightly toasted brioche in triangles. Lay them overlapping on the custard. Press them down. Ladle the rest of the custard over them. Stand in a hot water bath. Bake 30 minutes at 220°C.

unpizza

Suppose you've given up on shop bread and make your own, been making it for years. Sooner or later you'll stop measuring and start mixing the dough by feel. Maybe it will turn out fine, maybe too dense, maybe blow up like a soufflé. One day it will be too salty, another you'll forget the salt altogether. For a change, you'll add a handful of sunflower seeds, or switch your usual flour for spelt, or work in some olive oil, or switch the water for milk. Nobody said you were a professional baker – you just 'busk it' and hope something edible turns out, and that's an interesting word in itself with links to piracy, to ripping off whatever offers itself.

Another side-effect of this careless approach is that by accident or design, every so often you'll produce more dough than usual: too much for your tin, *banneton* or whatever shape or size your default loaf happens to be. This excess, like buccaneering, has history. In Provence, bakers tested the heat of their beehive ovens by tearing off scraps of dough and baking them, the *fougasses* they now sell as regional specialities. These are no different from the *focaccia* that evolved in the same way across the border in Italy. Pizzas, setting aside arguments pro and con their Neapolitan origins, belong to the same sisterhood.

Whenever surplus dough is going spare, it's potentially breakfast, lunch or snack: worth a tweet if turns out OK but no big deal. Dedicated cookery books or websites can detail the techniques and proportions for a *focaccia pugliese al rosmarino* with precision. However toothsome, it's only of peripheral interest. What matters is the here and now of what's to hand.

Because it's something extra, because it's not going to sit around for a day waiting to be eaten, its chief potential is as fresh crust. The crisper it is, the better it will taste. Forget whether the dough itself is white or brown, leavened with brewer's yeast or sourdough, just treat it like any flat-bread. Roll it out, rest it and flash it in a hot oven. Put something on top of it, any scraps from the fridge or larder that you fancy and it changes not so much into a pizza as an un-pizza, a spur-of-the-moment invention that needn't be aesthetically pleasing, that doesn't have to match up to some arbitrary standard of excellence. It's what it is.

So it won't be replicable. That's immaterial. Although many cooks depend on their personal repertoire whether in their heads or on paper, beyond a certain level of competence, as with any craft, they must feel instinctively that rules cease being rules. Nobody needs a handbook to make a sandwich. No more should anyone who routinely bakes his own bread feel constrained playing with the dough, least of all by his own ability.

Smearing duck rillettes on a slab of flatbread before baking it or dabbing it with segments of beetroot marinated in aged balsamic vinegar or crumbling some Stilton on it worked for me, that is, I think it did, once.

UN-PIZZA

60ml approx. olive oil • 150g approx. left-over bread dough
50g cooked sliced beetroot • 1 tsp good Balsamic vinegar
grated lemon zest • *herbes de Provence* • 100g sliced tomatoes
50g sliced courgette • coarse salt • pepper

Brush a baking sheet with most of the oil. Cover with rolled bread dough, about 27cm round. Leave to rise. Paint beetroot with balsamic vinegar. Preheat oven to 250°C. Put the beetroot on the dough, brush all with oil and bake 5 minutes. Sprinkle the other ingredients over the bread. Season aggressively. Brush with oil. Finish baking the flat-bread.

LEMON FLATBREAD

10g dried yeast • 200g unsalted butter • 210g bread flour
1 lemon • 1 beaten egg • 100g sugar • 10g melted butter

Dissolve the yeast in about 2tbs warm water. Soften 120g butter. Grate lemon zest. Knead together the yeast, softened butter, flour, grated lemon, egg and 30g sugar. Leave covered in a warm place 2–3 hours. Preheat oven to 230°C. Brush a baking sheet with melted butter. Knock back dough and spread by hand on the baking sheet. Aim for 25cm – 30cm circle. Squeeze lemon juice over it. Cube the rest of the butter and dot over the dough. Dust with sugar and bake 10–12 minutes. Turn up the oven temperature to maximum and glaze.

BREAD 'UN-RECIPE'

Our home-made bread isn't a fixed recipe, because we aren't professional bakers. It doesn't involve weighing or timing. It slots into the routine of our lives.

The sourdough leaven we use dates back to 1993. It lives in the fridge in a lidded Tupperware container. Sometimes it's frothy and bubbling over; sometimes it's heavy and sluggish. We keep it going by feeding it brown flour, white flour, spelt – whatever.

To make a loaf, we scoop or tear a good handful into a mixing bowl containing water at body temperature, salt and soft brown sugar or a spoonful of honey. How much water? We aren't precise: 400ml or 450ml for a large loaf; half a pint for smaller ones. Then we knead in just enough flour (or flours) to make a smooth dough, roughly the same amount as the water, perhaps a tad more.

Covered and left overnight the dough rises. Next day we knock it back and mould it. When it has risen again, we bake it in a hot, not *very* hot, oven. It won't help to give a temperature, because every domestic oven has its own quirks.

Consistency doesn't matter to us as it must do to a professional. We scratch our heads if a loaf seems a little doughy one day. We glow when it comes out of the oven perfect. We tinker with all the finer details that may affect the taste or texture. We go online or consult books for tips and tricks from other bread-makers.

AN ENGLISH 'TARTE FLAMBÉE'

300g left-over bread dough • 20g softened butter
110ml double cream • 110g cottage cheese
3 chopped spring onions • 80g lardons

Roll out the dough to an approximately 30cm. diameter circle. Lay it on a buttered baking sheet. Cover and leave to relax for an hour. Preheat the oven to 250°C. Bake for 5 minutes. Take out of the oven. Combine the cream, cottage cheese and onion. Spoon it over the bread – not quite to the edges. Sprinkle lardons on top. Finish baking, about 10 minutes more.

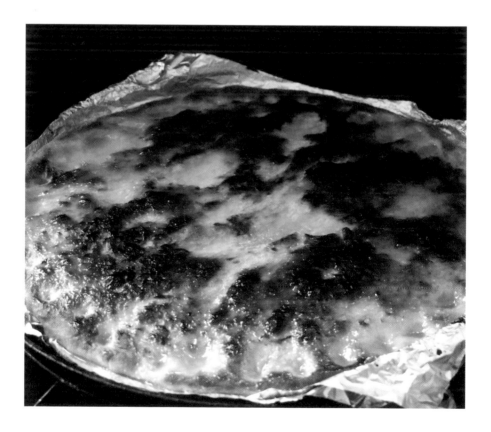

glop

...sticky and amorphous matter, typically something unpleasant: 'a cup of vile green glop'.

...a soft, shapeless lump of something: 'a glop of creamy dressing'.
Oxford Online Dictionary

Every self-respecting cook has a repertoire of dishes he or she is thoroughly ashamed of: tinned sardines mashed up with onions and vinegar; beetroot and Brie sandwiches; squashed hard-boiled eggs with tarragon and mayo; risotto with Cheddar cheese; soups concocted on the spur of the moment; oft-repeated combinations that never taste the same twice; aubergine gunk that tastes of its carelessly charred skin more than its flesh.

Created from what's to hand, be it in tin, jar, freezer or Tetrapak, food that's tricked out, careless of its appearance, let alone its nutritional value, demands almost nothing. It's for eating not analysing. What goes into the mix depends whether the cupboard is almost bare or whether it's overflowing. My most recent glop, call it 'Supper', was a mish-mash of onions, chicken livers, very old balsamic vinegar, tomato ketchup and Przyprawa (a cheap Polish [?] equivalent of Maggi).

The thing is, nobody had to justify it to anybody. It didn't come out of a book or even from a blog. Proportions? Doses? Haven't a clue. Knowing how to glop (the verb exists) is only open to those comfortable with ill-discipline.

AVO GLOP

salt • lime juice • 1 large avocado
1 red onion • 1 diced tomato
any or all of: mayonnaise, herbs, chilli, Worcester sauce

Dissolve the salt in lime juice. Add the avocado and mash roughly with a fork. Mix in the onion and tomato. Ring the changes with extra ingredients.

STEWED APPLE AND RASPBERRY

500g well-flavoured apples • approximately 180g sugar
500g raspberries • 1 sachet gelatine

Peel, core and chop the apples. Put them in a pan with very little water and the sugar. Stew until soft. Pass through a Mouli or sieve. Mash the raspberries and sieve to remove the seeds. Combine with apple and test for sweetness. Dissolve the gelatine powder in a little hot water. Whisk into the raspberry–apple mixture. Spoon into bowls and leave to thicken. The texture is more purée than jelly.

SMOKED HADDOCK CHOWDER

500g smoked haddock • 500ml milk • 60g butter
60g flour • 100ml dry cider • 250g peeled potatoes
200g sweetcorn kernels • salt and pepper
2tbs chopped parsley and chives

Put the haddock in an ovenproof dish and cover with milk. Microwave until flaking, about 5 minutes. Remove skin and any bones. Melt the butter in a pan. Stir in flour to make a roux. Add the cider. Whisk in the milk and simmer 10 minutes. Cut the potato into bite-sized pieces. Add to the sauce and continue simmering until cooked. Fold in haddock and sweetcorn. Check seasoning and finish with chopped herbs.

EGG, ROCKET AND LAND CRESS

6–7 hard-boiled eggs • salt and pepper • 60ml mayonnaise
60g finely diced onion • rocket to taste • land cress to taste

Shell and part mash the eggs. Season and fold in the mayonnaise. Add
the onion. Dice as finely as you can the stems of rocket and cress. Mix
in and add the leaves torn or shredded.

Use for sandwiches, open or closed.

CHICKEN LIVER STEW

30g butter or 30ml oil • 150g diced onion • 1 crushed garlic clove
350g chicken livers, cleaned of their gall • 2tbs tomato ketchup
1tbs soy sauce • ½ chicken stock cube
1tbs good balsamic vinegar • pepper

Heat the butter in a pan and brown the onions. Add the garlic and
then the chicken livers. Turn down the heat and stir. After a couple of
minutes, add ketchup, soy and crumbled stock cube. Go on stirring
until they're almost cooked through. Add vinegar and pepper.

BLACKCURRANT AND APPLE SNOW

700g 'wild' apples • 200g blackcurrants
250g approx. sugar • 2 egg whites

Peel, core and quarter the apples. Stew them in very little water
until they mush. Stew blackcurrants with 100g sugar until they start
splitting. Blend apples and blackcurrants in a food processor. Put the
rest of the sugar in a small pan with a splash of water. Whisk the egg
whites until well-risen. Boil the sugar to 115°C. Pour it on the egg
whites while whisking. Fold the fruit into the cooled meringue. Chill

patience

The ingredients list specifies a couple of pounds of braising steak. Step one of the method says: 'Heat the oil and brown the meat.' Can't take long, chuck it all in, sauté… yo, sorted – except it isn't. Beef cubes, packed like commuters in a rush-hour tube, don't move. Like them, they sweat. Flip them over and they're grey. Soon they're standing in a bubbling, cooking-juice swamp. It doesn't matter how hot the pan was to start with, it couldn't do the job; there was too much meat that probably came out of a shrink-wrapped package sitting in the bottom of the fridge.

Re-run the scenario. Unwrap the braising steak, pat it dry, heat a little oil in a large pan until it's almost smoking. Fry, virtually stir-fry the beef cubes a few at a time, until they're crisp and caramelized all over. When each little batch is coloured, empty the pan, heat a little more oil, tackle a few more pieces, until they're all done. It takes more messing around, granted, but the outcome is better. There's less frustration involved too. Watching meat turn grey instead of ruddy-brown, 'Ain't a pretty sight'.

The organic roast chicken's carcase lies in its death throes on the serving dish. It has no future except as stock. The conscientious cook drops it in a casserole, covers it with water, adds an onion, carrot and *bouquet garni*, simmers it all afternoon and into the evening. So why is it cloudy? Why does it taste like a wrung-out dishcloth?

Re-run the scenario. Chop the bones up small. Brown them in the oven along with the carrot and onions. Transfer them to a pot. Fill it up with cold water and bring it up to the boil. Skim any scum on the surface? Not essential. Add herbs and other aromatics? No hurry. Two hours later the broth smells of roast chicken soup. Why carry on cooking? Simply strain it. If it isn't strong enough, reduce it.

Slow food can be insipid. Fast food can taste scrumptious. Patience in a kitchen isn't about twiddling one's thumbs waiting for the custard to thicken. It's stirring it, watching it in case it begins curdling on a hot spot, sniffing the air for that unmistakable smell of cooked egg, milk, sugar and vanilla.

Of course 'Life's too short to peel a grape', or turn a mushroom, or clutter a plate with half a dozen redundant garnishes. No divine culinary law states, 'Thou shalt not use ketchup,' or HP sauce for that matter. If a sponge cake is lighter for whisking it over hot water and then whisking it some more until the mixture cools down, there's a case for doing it. Don't rest pastry after rolling it and it will shrink. Boil tagliatelle in too little water and it will be sticky whether it's hand-made or out of a packet. The reason for sharpening a knife isn't to chop faster, but better. Patience isn't time-driven, it's geared to a result.

SUMMER PUDDING

100g blackcurrants • 150g red currants • 200g sugar
600g raspberries and strawberries • 7 slices of diet white bread

Simmer blackcurrants with a cup of water for 5 minutes. Add red currants and sugar. Stir to dissolve. Bring to the boil and take off the heat. Empty them onto a sieve over a mixing bowl. Slightly crush red fruit with a fork. Add them to the sieve. Leave until the juices stop dripping. Cut up the bread to line a two-pint pudding basin. Taste the juice for sweetness and adjust to your preference. Line the basin with kitchen film. Dip pieces of bread in juice and line the basin's bottom and sides. Fill it with mixed fruit. Cover with the last of the bread. Weight the pudding and leave standing for at least 24 hours. Turn it out. Boil any left-over juice to a glaze and brush over the pudding.

SLOW-COOKED SHIN OF BEEF

DAY 1

1kg beef shin • 10g salt • 10g brown sugar • 2 bayleaves
2 star anis • 1 strip orange peel • 600ml red wine

Cut the shin into pieces weighing about 50g each. Rub salt and sugar over them. Leave 6 hours in the fridge. Make a marinade with the other ingredients and pour over the beef. Marinate overnight.

DAY 2

50 ml olive oil • beef from Day 1 • 50g flour
200g chopped onions • 200g roughly sliced carrots
60g celery • marinade from Day 1
1 beef stock cube • pepper

Heat the oil in a large pan until it smokes. Drain the meat and brown it a few pieces at a time. Transfer to the slow-cooker and coat thoroughly with flour. In the same pan, colour vegetables (add a touch more oil if necessary). Transfer to the slow-cooker. Pour some marinade into the pan and scrape sediment off the bottom. Transfer to the slow-cooker with the rest of the marinade. Add crumbled stock cube. Cover and slow-cook about 8 hours until the meat is tender. Season with plenty of pepper and maybe some extra salt.

RILLETTES

300g pork back fat • 15g salt • 700g pork belly without rind
300ml water • pepper

Rub the back fat with half the salt and cut it into cubes. Cut the pork belly into cubes. Start rendering the fat in a heavy bottomed pan. Add the meat and coat it in fat. Turn up the heat so the meat starts browning. Scrape the pan to prevent burning. Turn heat right down and add the rest of the salt. Pour in the water and cover pan with a tight-fitting lid. Simmer for 3 hours. Strain the fat and rendered juices into a bowl. Flake the meat with your fingers (don't mash it). Season with pepper. Beat in the fat and juice a little at a time. Reboil the meat and fat. Take off the heat and beat again while cooling. Leave to finish setting.

BONED AND ROLLED LEG OF LAMB

DAY 1

1 leg of lamb • 2 large garlic cloves
1tbs chopped rosemary • 100ml olive oil

The boning takes time. Lay the leg so the rounded surface is on the chopping board. You have to negotiate two big bones (femur and tibia). Depending on the butcher, you may have two other bones to remove. Cut off the knuckle end if it's still attached. Cut along the line of the shinbone (tibia). Expose the ball and socket join between shin and thighbone. Cut along the line of the thighbone (femur). The thigh may still be joined to the flatter aitch-bone. Use the point of the boning knife to cut around this. Keeping the knife-point against the bone, free the two big bones. Take special care around the 'knee joint' where they lock together. Open up the joint so the meat is exposed. Rub all the olive oil into it. Stud the muscle with spikes of garlic. Sprinkle rosemary over it. Rest overnight.

DAY 2

lamb from Day 1 • salt and pepper • 20ml olive oil

Preheat the oven to 190°C. Season the meat and roll it up. Tie it into a joint with string – but not too tightly. Brush with oil. Roast it, resting on the bones, over a roasting tin. When tested with a meat thermometer, it should be at 65°C core temperature for medium, or 70°C for well-done. Rest 10 minutes before carving.

Of course, you may be lucky and have the butcher bone the leg for you.

PORK AND CIDER TERRINE

DAY 1

100g streaky bacon • 12g salt • 3g pepper • 1tsp powdered sage
1tsp puréed garlic • 1 x 250g pork fillet
400g rare breed pork belly (no bones or rind) • 150g pig's liver
150ml good dry cider

Blend the bacon, salt, pepper, sage and garlic to a purée. Cut the pork fillet into 1cm cubes. Either coarse-mince the belly or chop it very fine by hand. Blend the liver in a food processor. Mix all the ingredients by hand and refrigerate overnight.

DAY 2

mixture from Day 1 • 300g thinly sliced streaky bacon rashers
2 bayleaves • sprig of sage

Take the mixture out of the fridge and knead for a minute. Line a terrine (1.25 litres) with bacon. (The strips should hang over the edges.) Preheat the oven to 130°C. Fill the terrine with mixture. Fold the bacon flaps over the top, and the herbs on top of that. Cover with foil or a lid. Stand the terrine in a bain marie with hot water half way up the sides. Bake in the oven for about 75 minutes. The ideal core temperature of the terrine is 69°C. Once out of the oven, put a weight on top of the terrine and leave for 24 hours in the fridge before turning out.

DID YOU ENJOY YOUR MEAL?

'Did you enjoy your meal?'

It was the question Roberto dreaded. He heard it, on average, between seven and eight times a week. The figure wasn't a guess; he'd kept a record for three statistically significant months.

Answering would not have been difficult except that he considered himself fastidious about his choice of words. He could fob off a waiter with an ambiguous 'Thank you', and a host (depending on the circumstances) with 'A charming evening', 'Entertaining', 'Interesting' or any other adjective that gave nothing away without actually being offensive.

His column had a dispassionate Zen-like quality to it. Unlike other critics who praised and panned according to the state of their digestion or prejudices, he wrote in an analytical clipped style where each phrase held the appropriate pertinence to its subject. His vocabulary had the same precision as a Master of Wine's.

If he described his turbot as 'fresh' that was because it retained the iodine taste of the sea. From there, allowing for synonyms, he would describe a downward spiral from 'bland' to 'stale' and finally 'putrid'.

'People do not read me for warmth, but for truth,' he had once told his editor, a decent sort who would happily have poisoned him.

The lady, sitting on his left, who had put the question, a TV celebrity on the crest of her first cookery series, didn't wait for his answer.

'It was mind-numbingly exquisite. You could taste every drop of the 40-year-old balsamic on the beetroot fettucine and the Bresse guinea fowl; well, Wow!'

Roberto pulled back the corners of his mouth in a rictus of a smile. The balsamic had barely left the cradle and if the guinea fowl came from Bresse, he was an Inuit.

Instead of correcting his neighbour's misconceptions directly, he already had enough enemies in his line of work, he pulled back the folds of his jacket, dipped his thumbs into a plum waistcoat and answered: 'Using the pipette to squeeze balsamic over beetroot to control the correct dosage isn't original, but is effective providing that the quality of the *aceto* merits it.' He paused, sniffed to imply his reservations, before continuing, 'I question, though, whether the beetroot (strong emphasis) hasn't been chosen more for its colour, than its flavour. By boiling, rather than baking it, the chef has missed an opportunity to contrast its natural earthiness with the relative sophistication of his concept.'

'Well, I liked it,' his neighbour, who wasn't short on confidence, retorted.

'Why shouldn't you?' joined in a large man opposite her.

Roberto could sense another storm brewing. Pietro Passolini wrote syndicated so-called criticism for a chain of regional newspapers. He looked like a turtle with his small beaked head emerging from a massive, rounded frame.

'I thought it was sublime,' he continued. 'You mustn't pay any attention to my friend Roberto. He eats like a mechanic. There's no passion in him.'

'Pietro,' he addressed the celebrity, 'belongs to the Pavarotti school of gastronomic reporters. Providing that he projects enough feeling in his work, he doesn't mind hitting a few false notes.'

'That's so charming, so human,' she replied, completely missing the point. 'It's my philosophy exactly. Wasn't it Escoffier himself who once said: *la femme cuisine comme l'oiseau qui chante*? That's how I am myself.'

'You must invite me to dinner in that case,' Pietro replied.

Roberto, seething at the woman's ignorance, twisted his napkin under the table.

It was one of those tricks of fate that affects professionals swimming in a small goldfish bowl. They can flap their tails in the same direction for months without meeting and then they can't avoid bumping into each other.

Roberto, wherever he dined, be it at the launch of a new improved frozen antipasti range, or at a hospitality industry exhibition, or at a dinner marking the visit of a world-famous chef, always found himself seated opposite or near Pietro Passolini. This he convinced himself was no accident. A strict hierarchy exists as to who sits where at such functions. Until quite recently, he had sat among the élite, whereas his colleague would be lost with other journeymen of his calibre in a corner of the room. Now, it appeared, his overweight, genial rival's star had surfaced at the second table, while he himself more often than not had sunk to it.

These meetings, however civil, were taking their toll on Roberto. He was not, he had long since realized, someone whom others liked. This hadn't troubled him because he took it for granted that they would always defer to him. Pietro challenged his identity on both fronts. Not only did he routinely throw doubt on his careful deconstructions, but the fellow insisted on being friendly too. To a Florentine intellectual, this could mean one thing only. His back was in danger of a painful stabbing.

The blow fell sooner than he had expected. It was autumn, the peak of the truffle season, when the *piazze* in the small Piedmontese town of Alba smell as sulphurous as the gates of Hades, when little men at street corners delve in their pockets for what look like lumps of clay and cost the earth.

Roberto loathed the annual market and fair held there, though he always attended, not for the cloying omnipresent scent of the fungus, nor the pervasive stench of *nouveau riche* money, nor even the contrived tapping, scratching and sniffing that accompanied whispered discussions which passed for negotiations, nor the endless speeches from the mayor or the president of a local association, or the famous face wheeled out to grin at the cameras, but for the way slippery waiters hovered over plates slicing truffles over every dish, at every meal, however inappropriate.

The ideal way to experience them, he had been telling his readers for as long as he could remember, was to shave four or five slices of a freshly gathered truffle over a freshly laid bantam egg fried gently in butter until just set.

At the grand gala dinner that climaxed the celebrations, he noted with satisfaction that the organizers had seated Pietro next to some foreigners, Germans he guessed, on one of the lower tables. It didn't, he realized, matter, but it felt like a victory. That evening, in his sparse and none-too-comfortable hotel room, he filed a story beginning, 'Why buy an Alba truffle for the price of a Fiat Punto?' It was quite, he felt, a humorous article. Perhaps he should compose others in that vein. Maybe he did take himself and his work too seriously.

His rival told another story, a better one. The Germans, it appeared, were guardians of a long-haired dachshund bitch which had inherited about €70 million. At the charity auction held to close the fair, she outbid a famous New York restaurateur for the largest truffle, paying enough for it to buy, if not a Ferrari, at least a top-of-the-range BMW. There was even a close-up of Bertha (that was her name) eating a rare steak topped with *tartufi bianchi* off a Dresden plate. Pietro had thoughtfully included a short recipe to accompany it.

It was the worst kind of tabloid journalism, but every major news agency picked it up.

Bertha was interviewed on Rai Uno news as well as by half a dozen lifestyle programmes. One of the colour supplements ran a series on dogs' dinners, featuring celebrity pets.

Of course, like Bertha, the story's legs were short. Jokes about truffle hounds subsided. Gastronomic columns reverted to the urbane monotony that kept the scribblers in employment without overtaxing the minds of their readers. Then it was that time of the year when contracts came up for renewal. After a very expensive lunch with his editor in Carlo Cracco's minimalist Milan tribute to the futurist cooking movement, Roberto realized that he had been fired, worse, that he had been ousted by the walking gut who couldn't string two sentences together.

He walked out of the restaurant with a feeling of emptiness, possibly because he had left most of the dishes he had been served uneaten – deconstructed, the apparently clever concepts hadn't proved a sufficient challenge to his palate to require more than a taste, probably because he hadn't prepared himself for an appropriate detached intellectual response to sacking, mainly because he could not find either the anger or the sense of shame that he felt he should be experiencing.

Instead of exercising at his health club, as he usually did in the afternoons, he returned to his apartment in a converted dress factory to face his future. It was an open-plan space dominated by bookshelves floor to ceiling that swaddled him from the world outside. He should, he knew, be in a state of shock, seasoned with the curry spices of emotional turmoil, the conventional response expected from those who are unexpectedly fired.?

After sipping a cup of Darjeeling sent him from London by a public relations company, he concluded he wasn't the type to go down that route. Like the British in a crisis, his lips would not quiver. In tranquillity, he would buy a small rucksack, book a ticket to Buenos Aires, vanish for a year and return with a masterpiece: 'Beefsteak From The Ashes'.

For dinner, he cooked himself *maccheroncini* with a little tomato sauce washed down with a wine from Le Marche with the unusual name of Chaos. A salad, a piece of *pecorino semi-secco*, a couple of hours of mindless television and he was ready for an early night.

He was flying, in the disjointed way that happens in a dream, an Alitalia Airbus over the Adriatic that dived into a mountain top in the Andes. At first he thought he was the sole survivor because there were no other passengers around him, merely the wrecked fuselage surrounded by the confetti of smashed luggage.

Sitting cross-legged beside him in the snow, though, was a pot-bellied, flabby, naked Buddha.

'What are you doing here Pietro?' he asked.

'Same as you.'

Overhead, Roberto heard the whir of helicopters searching for them.

'We'll be rescued soon,' he said.

'They stopped looking for us weeks ago.'

'We'll starve to death.'

'Don't worry, my friend, try this.'

Roberto noticed that Pietro had taken a butcher's knife and carved a large chunk of flesh from his thigh and handed it to him.

'Plenty more where that came from.'

He put the flesh in his mouth: 'Do you mind if I have another?'

'If you'd prefer, I could grill it for you.'

The smell of charcoal searing meat in the rarefied mountain air was exquisite.

'Plenty more where that came,' Pietro repeated when he saw that Roberto had finished wiping up the gravy on the plate with a crust of bread.

He ate, and ate and ate, devouring his rival until he had been reduced to a chubby, smiling face perched on top of a gleaming white skeleton.

'Did you enjoy your meal?'

'It was,' he hesitated, 'Of course I enjoyed it. It was just what I wanted.'

He looked about him. The plane had turned into a composite of every restaurant he had ever visited. Pietro sitting opposite him now was dipping his tie into a black sauce, squid ink most probably, and sucking the end.

'You're welcome to it, all of it,' he told the fat man, then he woke up.

Outside it was still dark though the early-morning traffic had started to build up. He couldn't, like Scrooge, claim a ghostly revelation that had turned him into a better human being, but he opened his eyes on a happier place than the one he had slept in. Having shaved and dressed he walked to a small market nearby, one he didn't usually visit because it wasn't the best in the city. There, he queued at a bar to breakfast on a *panino* and a cappuccino, something he never drank – the milk and froth were, gastronomically speaking, plebeian aberrations, before strolling through the aisles, stocking up on bread, fruit, salami and some fresh ricotta.

He wasn't sure what he was doing or why he was doing it. Impulses had never been his bag. It wasn't a new experience for him, more of a rediscovered one that linked him to a past where he hadn't orbited around the Planet Food. Back home, his purchases surprised rather than shocked him. He had bought apples because they were vermilion, whereas the food critic would have rejected them, knowing them to be tasteless. The salami was pre-sliced and, heresy of heresies, vacuum-packed. The ricotta came in a silver pack marked 'Made in Denmark'.

Mechanically, he switched on his TV, changing channels until, by chance, he hit on a cookery programme in which a young-looking mother was baking a microwave cake for her two putative teenage sons and their girlfriends. Roberto recognized her by her voice as the gushing woman whom he had sat next to months earlier. Her face had been plastered with a thick crust of make-up so she would appear younger that she was, almost unrecognizable from the real person who, he recalled, was divorced and had a grown-up daughter studying law.

With a sense of genuine pleasure he pointed the remote control at the screen and zapped her. He might have done exactly the same thing 24 hours earlier, but it would have been with a mixture of scorn and resentment. Now she was merely another face on the screen whom he didn't want to watch.

By the same token he could switch off the persona he had so carefully constructed for himself, someone so tightly held together he might have squeaked whenever he moved. Later, he promised himself, he would call Pietro to wish him well with the job. No doubt the fellow would make a better fist of it than he ever had. Maybe, Roberto thought, he could invite him out to dinner. He suspected he could never really like the man, but unless he gave it a try he would never find out.

INDEX